This wonderful book takes of battling a serious disease; at times so blunt it was difficult to read, and yet I can't imagine how hard it was to write. In such a forthright way, Susan shares with us her personal journal entries, candidly exposing her fears and anxieties, absence from family, and the huge responsibility of being her own health advocate. Bringing us face to face with the reality of our fragile lives, her steadfast faith in the shadow of such turmoil serves to encourage and uplift. Her honesty is both brave and disarming, and I was surprised by how inspiring and affirming an account of suffering and hardship can be.

—**Jayma Mays**, actress

Susan Parris's book on her battle with cancer is an amazing, encouraging journey. Her trust in God and love of her family is something that touched my life, as my mother experienced the same voyage. Susan does an amazing job painting the picture of the roller coaster of this disease and how an unwavering faith is the key to victory. Her relentless faith in Christ is the narrative thread that makes this story UTTERLY AMAZING!

—**Ryan O'Quinn**, actor, author
Parenting Rules! and *Marriage Rules!*

"You have cancer" are the three most terrifying words that one can hear. *Cancer Mom* is a story of a young mother's journey through the confusion, pain, loss of control, and the fear of death that comes hand-in-hand with a breast cancer diagnosis. Susan's vivid portrayal of her fear at the initial diagnosis, confusion about which treatment to pursue, and the pain of leaving behind loved ones, especially young children, to seek treatment made me feel so many familiar emotions—it was as if I was living the experience all over again. Her reliance on her faith in God and His teachings will give courage, comfort, and hope to those who struggle with the chance to live life, and to live it even better than before.

—**Sandy McGlothlin**, inflammatory breast cancer survivor
patient, MD Anderson Cancer Center

Cancer Mom

Cancer
Mom

Hearing God in an
Unknown Journey

SUSAN
PARRIS

POINTE PRESS

Disclaimer

This book is licensed for your personal enjoyment and education only. Nothing in this book should be construed as personal advice or diagnosis, and must not be used in this manner. The information in this book should not be considered as complete and does not cover all diseases, ailments, physical conditions, or their treatment. You should consult with your physician regarding the applicability of any information provided herein and before beginning any healthcare program or counseling. This book is not intended to provide healthcare facility, provider, or treatment recommendations, nor is it intended to discredit or disparage any healthcare facility or provider or treatment plan.

This book is a recollection of events, which the author has related to the best of her knowledge. Some identities have been changed or are composites to maintain their anonymity. The conversations in the book all come from the author's recollections, though they are not written to represent word-for-word transcripts. Rather, the author has retold them in a way that evokes the feeling and meaning of what was said and in all instances, the essence of the dialogue is accurate.

For Briggs and Glenn,

*That you might know me better and
understand how much I love you.*

October 26

I came home and put my children to bed. I lay down with Briggs on one side and Glenn on the other. I read them a book. We said a prayer together.

The boys both prayed, "Dear God, help Mommy's boo-boos get better."

Tears streamed down my face, but I made sure neither child saw them. I kissed their faces and put my arms around them both until they drifted off to sleep.

My eyes circled the room. I could hear the Thomas-the-Train clock ticking. I wished I could stay right there between them forever.

Contents

Introduction

"Nothing to Worry About"

"You have nothing to worry about." The words from my doctor didn't console me. He didn't realize what my life was like when he spoke those words that continued to banter around in my mind. My oldest son was five years old and beginning kindergarten—high stress for a young mother who'd convinced herself that kindergarten success was the key to my dreams for his life.

After getting my son acclimated to Mrs. Stanley's kindergarten class, and with my youngest son in preschool, I turned my attention once again to the doctor's words— "nothing to worry about." The tiny spot on my chest and the pain under my arm were still causing sleepless nights, and I wondered if it could be something serious. Not worrying proved to be a difficult prescription to fill.

Looking Back

During this time of "not worrying," Stan and I were getting ready to celebrate our twelfth wedding anniversary. We'd met in the ninth grade at Waynesville Junior High School in North Carolina. Standing beside my locker after fourth-period science, Stan asked me to the ninth-grade dance. I bought a pink Jessica McClintock dress for the special occasion. Stan showed up at my doorstep in white pants, white shoes, and a North Carolina Tar Heel blue blazer. The wrist corsage he had for me was a little large, but at the moment I was thrilled that it wasn't the cheap kind he had to pin on. Stan had talked his older brother into chauffeuring us in his parents' green van. The '80s were so cool! We survived the dance, not realizing that one day we would celebrate twelve years of marriage.

Stan and I dated on and off for the next eight years. Our lives took different paths after high school. I attended the University of Georgia and Stan went to the University of Tennessee. After the first few years of college, our off-and-on relationship started getting more serious and expensive. It's hard to believe we survived the long-distance dating scene without cell phones, texting, email, or Facebook. I remember the excitement of getting a handwritten letter from Stan in my mailbox, or a surprise phone call on a weekend night. One of those calls came on Saturday night during our senior year of college. Stan had been for a long walk around the Knoxville campus. He called to share with me that God was leading him to attend seminary in Texas. Later, I discovered the consequences of that late-night decision.

Football is king at Georgia. With all the southern flair possible, the games "between the hedges" are major events. The students are dressed in formal wear, while the team's bulldog mascot roams the sidelines in a stadium transformed into a sea of red. The famous hedges outlining the field are as famous as Bulldog players, such as Herschel Walker. Each fall, my friends and I planned our schedules around the Saturday games.

Stan came for a weekend visit in October 1991. The weekend was going to be exciting with him visiting and Georgia playing Clemson. Stan arrived on Friday night, and we drove out to one of the most beautiful spots on the North Campus. Under a tree, Stan got down on one knee and asked me to marry him. Just like my answer when he asked me to the ninth-grade dance, I now said yes to his marriage proposal. Stan carved our initials in the tree where he asked me to marry him.

On September 5, 1992, we were married. The vows we made to each other that day included our promise to be committed to each other "in sickness and in health," something we would be challenged to keep in a few short years.

The wedding day was filled with fun and great memories. Our outdoor reception was accompanied by rain, and lots of it. They say rain is supposed to bring you good luck on your wedding day. I don't know about that, but it made for some good memories to talk about through the years.

The Texas Years

After spending the fall in North Carolina, we said goodbye to our families and moved to Fort Worth, Texas, where Stan attended Southwestern Baptist Theological Seminary to prepare for the ministry. The move was hard. I never imagined I would live so far away from my family. If I had to describe those years in one word, it would be poor. But now as I think about those years, maybe I should use the word prepare.

Newly married and moving a thousand miles away from my family created some newlywed tension. Looking back, I see God was preparing us for what was ahead in my life. Stan and I grew close and developed an independence that was healthy for us. More important, we learned how to make decisions on our own. The three years we spent in Texas prepared us not only for the ministry, but also for life. In fact, the growth that occurred during those difficult years played a key role later when I faced the challenge of a lifetime.

I'm not sure if anything can fully prepare a person for the ministry, particularly for being a pastor's wife. I knew God had called Stan and me to the ministry, but I wasn't sure what my role would be. Being a part of a pastor's family has unique blessings and struggles. Seeing God change lives is what keeps ministers and their families going when they're feeling the stress of ministry.

Through the early years of ministry, Stan and I visited with many people and enjoyed invitations for dinner in many homes. On several occasions, we visited and prayed with someone who was battling cancer. Our prayers were genuine and our concern was real—but we had no idea what these people were really dealing with, or what it meant to cope with the pain and fear of cancer.

Remote in Appalachia

We arrived at Vansant Baptist Church in southwestern Virginia in September 1995 filled with excitement and enthusiasm. The sleepy coal-mining town suffered hard times from unemployment due to several large mines closing. Jobs were scarce, and hope dwindled. Yet we sensed a genuine love there that we'd never felt before.

Stan was off to work with dreams of building a great church. I was left at home wondering where in the world I was. The closest Walmart was an hour-and-a-half away. I traveled two hours to a hospital to deliver my children. While Texas is flat and hot, southwest Virginia is filled with steep mountains and deep valleys, which served as a reminder of how life seemed to be there.

Our early years at the church were busy and challenging. We desired to reach people and grow the church, but it was a tough task, considering the number of people who were leaving town due to the economy. As we served throughout the years, God blessed us with some tremendous friendships that would prove to be invaluable for the storm that was fast approaching.

Nine years after we were called to Vansant, we had an opportunity to leave for a bigger church in a larger town. From the outside, it looked like an easy decision. Our families and our friends outside the church were telling us to go, and at first we thought we would. After agonizing about the decision, in the end we decided to stay in Vansant.

God's Word was pivotal in our decision. We sensed God giving us a clear message from the small Old Testament book of Haggai:

> This is what the LORD Almighty says: "These people say, 'The time has not yet come to rebuild the LORD's house.'"
>
> Then the word of the LORD came through the prophet Haggai: "Is it a time for you yourselves to be living in your paneled houses, while this house remains a ruin?"
>
> Now this is what the LORD Almighty says: "Give careful thought to your ways. You have planted much, but harvested little. You eat, but never have enough. You drink, but never have your fill. You put on clothes, but are not warm. You earn wages, only to put them in a purse with holes in it."
>
> This is what the LORD Almighty says: "Give careful thought to your ways. Go up into the mountains and bring down timber and build my house, so that I may take pleasure in it and be honored," says the LORD. "You expected much, but see, it turned out to be little.

What you brought home, I blew away. Why?" declares the LORD Almighty. "Because of my house, which remains a ruin, while each of you is busy with your own house." (Haggai 1:2–9)

Have you ever felt regret after making a decision? Stan and I thought that our opportunity to move was perfect for us to fulfill our goals for our family and for our careers. But, through Haggai, God told us to stay where we were. Instead of building a new house for myself, God's plan for us was to help build a new church in Vansant. I didn't understand this decision at the time. I felt dreary and empty, like the cold, February weather.

I'd been saving a new pair of shoes I'd bought to wear on our first Sunday at the new church. Now I walked into worship at Vansant wearing those shoes, feeling like a great opportunity had just walked by my life. Soon, however, I would discover the power of God's sovereignty. He had a plan. He always does.

This experience was building a foundation to teach me two truths about life. One, God's Word is powerful and He speaks to us through His Word. Second, friends are essential in the journey of life. I would need both in just a few short months. God would once again speak to me through an Old Testament prophet and use my deep friendships in utterly amazing ways.

Eight months after making the decision to stay at Vansant, I heard the words I'll never forget, words no human being wants to hear. Earlier the doctor had said, "You have nothing to worry about." But on October 20, 2004, the doctor said, "You have cancer."

1

The Day of Small Things

Who despises the day of small things?

ZECHARIAH 4:10

"Beep, beep, beep!" The alarm sounded on a Monday morning. It was time to roll out of bed and begin a new week. I often wonder why we use an "alarm" to start out the day.

A Discovery

In my mind, the plans for the week seemed routine. As I stood in the shower, I mentally scrolled through the items that needed to be accomplished that day. There was the usual kids' stuff, a hectic work schedule, and trying to map out the meals for the week.

As I towel-dried, I felt a tiny knot on my chest. I paused and began to feel over my chest again and again. It felt almost like a little bone spur attached to my chest bone.

The clock turned to 7:30, and it was time to get the kids up for breakfast. I often wondered what I did with all my time before my children were born. The daily routine had started.

One week later I still felt the knot. Some days I couldn't feel it, but if I focused and rubbed over my chest enough times, I eventually found it. It felt about the size of a tiny peppercorn or a little BB. The knot was below my collarbone, so I wasn't sure what to think.

I kept telling myself to not be so paranoid. Drama is not my thing. I decided I should probably call my gynecologist. I was sure he would tell me just to watch it, and he would look at it when I came for my regular appointment.

Instead, the doctor suggested I come in immediately for a consultation. An appointment was scheduled for the next day. I was embarrassed because I didn't know if the little knot was in my breast or on my chest bone. I knew I should have taken an anatomy class. But my education had centered around economics and business.

Getting My Attention

I've always heard that it's the little things you need to pay attention to. I was in the routine of thinking about the future—my kids, my dreams, and my career. But this little knot, so small I could barely feel it, would impact every area of my life.

Sometimes, a small thing can have greater impact than a major event. Zechariah, the prophet, rebuilt the foundation of the temple of the Lord. Seventeen years passed, and now the people were referring to that work as a small thing. But Zechariah asks, "Who despises the day of small things?" (Zechariah 4:10). Many viewed that rebuilt foundation as a small thing. But to God, small things are important.

A brief article making the rounds on the Internet tells of various small things on September 11, 2001, that meant the difference between life and death for certain people who worked in the Twin Towers at the World Trade Center in New York City. Various circumstances caused some people to be late for work that morning—things such as an alarm clock that didn't go off, or a car that wouldn't start, or getting stuck in traffic because of an accident, or missing a bus. These people were spared that day, while the lives of so many others were tragically lost.

God often speaks to us through the small things. The knot on my chest was small. But through that small knot, God was speaking.

Often, the small things are overlooked, forgotten, or considered insignificant. And if we're honest, it's the small things—such as the spilled drink, the tired child, the flat tire, the forgotten file for work—that seem to annoy us so much because they take us away from our routine and schedule. But could it be that God is speaking to us through those small things?

I arrived at the doctor's office ready to get this small knot taken care of so I could get back to my routine. The doctor asked me to direct him to the place where I felt the knot. After careful examination, he concurred that it was quite small, but he didn't want me to leave until we knew exactly what it was. He referred to it as a "lump" and explained that, even though it was high on my chest wall, breast tissue extends to the collarbone.

I was immediately scheduled for an ultrasound and mammogram.

This small thing continued to be an interruption in my life.

2

October 20

I was headed to the department of horror—mammography! At least that was what I'd always heard about it.

According to insurance guidelines, I wasn't old enough to have annual mammograms. I put on a white gown and sat in a waiting room with two older ladies. They were so different from me, for I was young and healthy. I thought, *What am I doing here?* It was a question I would repeat many times during the next eighteen months.

I buried myself in a magazine, not wanting to talk to the other ladies. They began discussing a discount shoe store near where I live. I became so interested in their conversation that time quickly passed.

"Susan Parris?"

I was startled when they called my name, having been absorbed in the shoe conversation I was overhearing.

I was escorted into a small, dimly lit room. The technician explained how she would apply pressure to the breasts and then take pictures. She asked me to take a deep breath and not exhale while the pictures were being taken.

The procedures were quickly over, and I concluded that the horror ascribed to mammograms is overrated.

Unimagined Conversations

Have you ever been in conversations that you never thought you would have?

I found myself talking with the lady administering the ultrasound and having a conversation I thought could possibly happen only far down the road—perhaps twenty-five years down the road. The ultrasound technician said that cancer usually has tentacles or distortions, and that my spot was perfectly round. I was so thankful my "lump" wasn't like everybody else's. My husband has always told me I was different.

I reported back to Dr. G.'s office where he went over the reports. He calmly told me that according to the mammogram and ultrasound report, the lump didn't appear to be cancerous. However, he wanted me to consult with a surgeon, just to be on the safe side. He made me an appointment for later in the day with a friend of his. I was grateful, because I didn't want to make the two-hour trip back to see the surgeon.

After a quick lunch, I went see the breast surgeon. I knew very little about him, but I did know some women who had been patients of one of his partners, and they were pleased. Dr. G. had assured me this was the place to go in our region.

When I arrived at the surgeon's office, the waiting room was packed with mostly older people. I said a quick prayer of thanks that no one I knew was there. I didn't want the news getting back to Vansant that Susan Parris had been to see a breast surgeon!

After I'd filled out the new patient paperwork, my name was

called, and I was escorted to an examining room. The surgeon walked in, and we exchanged brief introductions. He did a breast exam and told me he'd reviewed the mammogram and ultrasound.

"I feel confident this is a fibroadenoma," he said. "You have nothing to worry about. They can stay in your body for years."

He showed me the picture on film, noting how the lump was perfectly round, and that the ultrasound picked up no echoes. He told me it wasn't uncommon for women my age to have fibroadenomas in their breasts. I asked him to spell the word at least three times, as well as pronounce it.

Pivotal Question

Wanting to cover all my bases, I asked about a biopsy.

"There's nothing there to biopsy," he replied. "The tumor is solid. There's no fluid."

If only I'd known then what I know now.

The surgeon also reminded me that I had no family history of breast cancer. Only later would I learn that 80 percent of women diagnosed with breast cancer have no family history of the disease.

I left the doctor's office relieved. I was deeply appreciative of the doctors who had worked so hard to fit me into their schedules in such a timely manner to ensure the well-being of my health.

I got back into my van and called Stan. I gave him the diagnosis of fibroadenoma. I knew he would at once see what he could find on the Internet. I relaxed for a moment and a wave of relief crossed over me. Then, I embarked on my two-hour trip back home to Vansant.

A week later, I recommended this doctor to a dear friend.

Six Weeks Later

It became my morning ritual to check this small lump on the upper part of my chest. It was always there, a tiny, hard, round lump. As I looked in the mirror that particular morning, it occurred to me the lump was growing. I called my gynecologist and scheduled another visit.

He concurred that he thought it might be growing. He asked when I was scheduled to see the surgeon again. I had an appointment in six weeks. The gynecologist saw no need to go sooner, and I left feeling confident that if he'd had any concern, he would have immediately sent me to the surgeon.

It was summer, and I tried to absorb every minute of it with my two sons—especially since my oldest, Briggs, would begin kindergarten in the fall. How do children grow up so quickly? Time evaporates like the morning dew.

Like many mothers, I struggled about where to send my children to school. At the time, I felt like this single decision would determine the fate of my children's success in life.

Meanwhile, my summer schedule was packed with swim lessons, Vacation Bible School, and trips to North Carolina to be with grandparents.

Summer quickly faded. I discussed the lump with my parents. My mom quickly informed me that my aunt had a fibroadenoma when she was my age, and thus, that must be what I had. No one seemed to be concerned, so why should I?

Stan and I planned a trip to the beach at the end of July. We'd saved all year for this vacation. It would be our first year to spend an entire week at the beach, one of my favorite places in the world. It's one of the few locations where I feel totally relaxed, and the kids love it.

I began writing in a journal—something I'd always wanted to do but never found the time. Later, I would see how God had a plan for my journal.

July 30

Pizza and ice cream at the docks at Bohicket Marina was the setting last night. Fishing poles in hand, Briggs and Glenn each caught a fish. Wow! What a perfect ending to our last night at the beach. This was the first time the boys had caught a fish at the beach. What a relaxing evening, sitting at the marina watching the boats and the ocean as the sun goes down.

This morning the boys are examining all their sea shells. Some shells look perfect and beautiful. One was broken. Bleached white from the sun, but yet so pretty. Another one was large and very weathered. You could see where the ocean and elements had worn holes into it over time. It had character.

How appropriate this morning when I read Proverbs 3:11. "My son, do not despise the Lord's discipline and do not resent his rebuke, because the Lord disciplines those he loves, as a father the son he delights in."

Even though the shell was broken, it was beautiful. Even though the shell was weathered with holes, it had character. Thank you, Lord, for time at the beach. Thank you for speaking to me.

Time spent at the beach—precious memories!

Wearing a bathing suit, I looked at myself in the mirror. I realized the lump was growing. I could see it in the mirror. It was so easy to find. Two months earlier I could hardly find it, even by touch. I promised myself I would have it checked again soon.

We returned from the beach, and Briggs started kindergarten. How can beginning kindergarten be so stressful on a mom? I felt so burdened. Why?

August 2

> Briggs's first day of kindergarten. Didn't we just bring him home from the hospital? How is it possible? School starts so early and there are still several things I wanted us to do this summer. God, give Stan and me wisdom and guidance to make the right decisions regarding our children.
>
> I anxiously pick Briggs up from school. "Mom, I learned all my vowels! A, E, I, O, U!"
>
> Briggs, it's your first day of school.

Still burdened for my children, I drew closer and closer to God and spent more time in prayer and reading my Bible.

A week after kindergarten started, Stan left for his first international mission trip. I felt his anxiety about leaving us and the long flight ahead. I was excited for him, although managing the kids without him is always challenging.

One day I dropped Briggs off at school and took Glenn to the babysitter's. I had a meeting at work that day, so I was dressed up more than usual. After I dropped Briggs off, I overheard his teacher say, "Briggs, your mother looks so pretty today. Why is she so dressed up?" Briggs responded, "My dad's in Trinidad!" What a response from the preacher's son!

Clouds on the Horizon

Everything just seemed so busy. Stan's ministry work was thriving while he tried to complete his doctorate degree by studying late into the night. My job became increasingly demanding as the bank undertook a name change. Briggs had started kindergarten, and Glenn would start preschool just a few weeks later. Change was everywhere.

The tumor was changing too. It continued to grow. It was now visible to the eye. I had a growth on my chest!

I woke up in the middle of the night with pain under my arm. Could this be related?

On September 6, I went see the surgeon again. He examined me but didn't seem concerned. Again he said I had nothing to worry about. "Fibroadenomas can grow just like this."

While his words were comforting, I felt concerned. I mentioned the pain under my arm, and he told me it wasn't related.

He asked if it hurt to touch the lump.

"No, not right now." I told him I wanted it removed and taken out of my body, no matter what it was.

"It's too early for another ultrasound," he replied.

When I persisted, he cautioned me that where the lump was located, the surgery would definitely leave a visible scar. "You should think about that. You'll be able to see the scar anytime you wear a V-neck shirt."

What Do I Do?

He scheduled me to come back in December for a follow-up ultrasound. I left his office feeling stressed and dissatisfied, while at the same time comforting myself with his words, "You have nothing to worry about."

As I drove home, I decided I wouldn't be going back there again. I was going to get another opinion. Who or where, I didn't know.

I placed the December appointment card down deep into my wallet.

The next day I called my gynecologist, who I felt was the only person who could help me. I spoke with his nurse and told her my concerns. She suggested that I see the surgeon's partner. Not an option for me. I was going somewhere else. But where?

I lay in bed not knowing what to do. *Who do I talk to?* I certainly didn't want it all over town that I was having a fibroadenoma taken out of my breast. I was a pastor's wife in a small town; the fact that my breasts would be other people's lunch conversation horrified me.

I prayed.

Life continued onward, like a train in a subway.

Stan and I were busy that month leading conferences for Virginia Baptists. The conferences were fun and rewarding, but, like anything in life, also time-consuming. I felt so drained and tired.

Paths Cross

After church on Sunday, September 20, God answered my prayer. I found Dr. Sutherland standing alone on the church steps. As much as I didn't want to discuss my concern, here was my opportunity to seek help. I quickly approached him and told him I had a little place I needed to have removed and needed to know of a good surgeon. He gave me the name of a doctor in Kingsport, Tennessee.

I called the following morning and got the first available appointment with Dr. E. on October 12. I'd made up my mind: this thing was coming out.

In the meantime, I planned my schedule for being out of work for a couple of weeks. I decided I could use a couple of weeks off. A little time of rest sounded like a good idea for my body. I'd never had surgery, and the thought of it was a little frightening.

October 5

The last two months have been difficult for me regarding Briggs's school. I feel so burdened for my children. May I continually affirm that God loves my children more than I can, and that He is keenly interested in their well-being.

As I read the book of Exodus, how connected I feel to the children of Israel. How I always look back, never satisfied with the blessings and miracles of God today. May I stay focused on where God is leading me.

October 12 finally arrived, and I headed to Kingsport, Tennessee, to see Dr. E. He reviewed my ultrasound and mammogram from May and did a physical exam.

I told him I wanted it out. He agreed and told me he thought he could perform the surgery and not leave a noticeable scar. I welcomed that news, and thought, *Doctor, where have you been?*

But first he wanted to perform a biopsy. I quickly responded that I'd wanted a biopsy earlier, but my previous doctor had said no. Dr. E. explained the difference between core biopsy and needle biopsy procedures. I didn't know there were two different types. The core biopsy is performed on solid tumors to examine the tissue. He scheduled me for such a biopsy two days later.

Life seemed so busy. My mother's birthday was that weekend, and I was headed to North Carolina to celebrate. I felt guilty enough living so far from my family, so I'd committed that the kids and I would go back for all their special occasions.

I went home and tried to convince Stan that a biopsy was no big deal and I could go by myself—while inside I was scared to death. How bad was this going to hurt? The surgeon's nurse told me, "It shouldn't be too bad." What else can they tell you?

On October 14, Stan and I traveled to Tennessee for the biopsy. I lay on the table as the doctor explained the procedure. Then he began using an ultrasound Doppler to look at the lump. He moved the wand repeatedly over my left breast. He then examined the film from May and pointedly asked, "Where was this film taken?"

"Here," I replied, "at this hospital."

He continued reviewing the ultrasound, then again moved the Doppler over my breast. Next he excused himself from the room, saying he needed to call my surgeon. My mind told me something was wrong, but my heart said, "Don't panic or overreact."

The doctor returned. "I'll be doing several core biopsies today," he stated. When I asked why, he responded, "There's more than one place of concern."

He had a difficult time getting one of the biopsies, and it was painful. When the procedure was finished, he placed his hand on my forearm and said, "You did very well today. I hope everything's okay. But if it's not, I hope the Lord gives you the strength to get through it."

The chill of his words rushed through my body as ice was applied to my painful breast. Fear and numbness unexpectedly slapped me in the face.

I quickly turned and looked him in the face. With my public-relations smile I said, "Thank you. I appreciate that."

Tears of Truth

Those last words he spoke to me continued to echo in my mind. It was if he already knew the diagnosis.

I was ushered into the dressing room, then out to the waiting room where Stan was seated. As soon as our eyes meet, I wanted to fall into his arms and cry. I was scared, and I was in pain.

As he quickly approached me, I looked at him and snapped, "Do not ask me anything until we get outside in the car." The last thing I wanted was to have someone see me falling apart in the middle of the hospital.

I shut the car door and began crying. It was the first time since this little tumor revealed itself five months earlier that I thought, *I might have cancer.* I knew the lump was something, but I never thought it was cancer.

Stan tried to console me, but my mind was focused on the doctor's words and the look on his face when he told me he hoped everything was okay, but if not, he hoped the Lord gave me strength to get through it.

Stan assured me that everything would be okay. "Susan, no one in your family has breast cancer," he encouragingly repeated.

I decided to tell a couple of my close friends about the events of the day. I wanted and needed them to pray for me.

The next day I drove four hours to North Carolina with the boys to celebrate my mom's birthday. I was so sore. I tried to remove the biopsy experience from my mind. I knew I could do nothing about it. I just had to wait until I heard from the doctor. Besides, this weekend was about Mom, and I wanted it to be special for her.

We went shopping most of Saturday. One of my best friends from high school was getting married in November in Raleigh. While buying outfits for the wedding, I also found a black V-neck shirt. I told myself, "You'll have this lump removed, and in a month, life will be back to normal. And you'll be wearing a new V neck with no scar showing!"

Monday came and I heard nothing. On Tuesday I called the doctor's office throughout the day, but I never spoke with the doctor.

I took the boys to a ballgame that evening to see their friend Keegan play. The doctor phoned our home while we were gone, and I missed his call.

At the game, my friend, Becky, asked if I'd heard anything. I said no. I let her feel the lump. Her eyes looked frightened. She was shocked at how big it felt—and so was I. It was really swollen after the biopsies. She was the first person I'd ever let feel it, outside of Stan, my mom, and the doctors.

I went to sleep remembering the look on Becky's face.

Finding Out

I was in my office at TruPoint Bank when Becky emailed me at 9:00 a.m.: *Have you heard from the doctor?*

I didn't want to call him. I didn't really want to know. I assumed it was a bad sign that no one at his office could talk to me about it.

I called. Again I got the nurse. She told me they had the report back, but I would have to talk to the doctor. She suggested I come over.

Kingsport was more than two hours away. I told her I wanted to know now. She hesitated.

Then I said, "I have cancer."

"Yes," she responded. "You have breast cancer."

3

One Lived, One Died

Spring brings tornado season across the South. The destruction and devastation can be massive, with hundreds injured or losing their lives, and even more losing their homes.

Carson Tinker was a member of the Alabama Crimson Tide football team. He was in Tuscaloosa when the tornado of April 2011 hit. As reported in *Sports Illustrated* that May, Carson was lifted out of his apartment by the tornado and thrown a hundred yards—the length of a football field. He suffered a concussion and blacked out.

Carson's girlfriend, Ashley Harrison, had been with him. In fact, as the tornado approached, Carson was huddled over her in a closet, holding on to her and trying to shield her from the devastating storm. He tried with all his human strength, but Ashley was ripped from his arms.

After coming to his senses, Carson wandered through the wreckage everywhere and screamed, "Ashley, where are you? Ashley!" But she was gone—her life taken by the tornado.

Both these young people were in the same storm, both in the same place. One was taken; one was left. One lived; one died.

Cancer seems to work in this random pattern, picking and choosing its victims. You sit in a room with others waiting for your name to be called. You have the test done, then you wait. One person learns she does not have cancer, and she rejoices. The person who was sitting next to her does have cancer, and she's heartbroken.

One person survives cancer. Another person does not. How does God decide?

In the greatest sermon ever preached, Jesus said that God "causes the sun to rise on the evil and good, and sends rain on the righteous and the unrighteous" (Matthew 5:45). When it comes to cancer, it seems like cancer affects the healthy and the unhealthy alike, young and old alike, sinners and saints alike.

Notes Amid Numbness

Nothing in life prepares you to learn that you have cancer.

After confirming my suspicions on that October day, the nurse on the phone asked me, "Are you okay? We don't like to talk about this over the phone."

I grabbed a legal pad and said, "I'm fine. Now, tell me everything you know." As she shared the information with me, I wrote it down.

I was thirty-four years old. I had no family history of cancer and no risk factors. I considered myself a very healthy person. I breastfed each of my two children for a year.

My children were three and five years old. How could this be happening? Just like a tornado taking one life and leaving the other, why did I get chosen?

I emailed Becky to let her know what the nurse had told me over the phone.

About 9:30, Stan walked into my office. How do you tell the

soul-mate of your life that you have cancer? I didn't know the answer. I just looked at him and whispered, "It's cancer."

No sooner had the words left my mouth than a coworker came into my office and began talking with us. He made a joke about how serious we seemed, so I put on a fake smile and laughed it off. After what seemed like an eternity, he finally quit talking and moved along.

Stan came over to me and said, "Let's get out of here."

I responded, "I can't." I had a meeting with senior management thirty minutes later, and I had important information to go over. I couldn't leave.

I began a mental conversation with myself. "Don't think about it. You've got to get through this workday. Just act like everything is normal."

After that work meeting was over, I asked my boss, the bank president, if I could speak with him. I began telling him I was sick and would need surgery in the near future. I mustered the strength to say the words out loud: "I have cancer."

Immediately, the conversation fell silent. It was a nervous silence that I always struggle with. I tried to fill the gap with some kind of conversation. I begin explaining to him that I was angry because I'd gone to a doctor months earlier who told me I had nothing to worry about.

I couldn't believe I was having this conversation with the president of the bank. I don't think that he could believe it either. He began discussing all the things that needed to be taken care of at the bank. We finished talking, and I asked him not to say a word to anyone. He agreed and kept his word.

At lunchtime, I went home.

The Doctor Search

Stan meanwhile had quickly gone to see a dear friend who had battled breast cancer herself nine years prior. He wanted her to know about me, and he also wanted to get information about the doctor she'd seen. She advised Stan to go by and see Dr. Clint Sutherland, a local internist, and the man who had initially directed me to Dr. E. Ironically, on the previous Sunday at church, Clint had said to Stan, "You've been a big help to me. If there's ever anything I can do for you, please let me know." Clint proved to be an immediate help.

We had family in North Carolina and were familiar with Duke Hospital there, so Stan thought that this would be a good first option for me. He mentioned this to Dr. Sutherland, who quickly made connections. By the end of that day, I had appointments at Duke Hospital for the following Tuesday and Wednesday.

At home for my lunch break from work, I was scared. I didn't want to die. What would my children do? In the middle of my crying, a thought jolted me: *I can't die. I only have a tiny life insurance policy. What will happen to my family?*

My brother, Brian, had tried to get me to increase my life insurance a month earlier. I deferred and told him we could do it over Thanksgiving when my existing policy was due for renewal.

As I sat in tears in the bathroom, I decided to call Brian. "Help me," I asked him. "I have to get life insurance immediately."

Brian tried to console me and told me I wasn't going to die. He shared with me that since I'd already been diagnosed, life insurance wasn't an option for me. I begged him to please get on the phone and try.

As I collected my emotions, I also asked Brian if he would tell my parents about my diagnosis. I didn't think I could tell them myself; I needed him to do it for me. I couldn't bear the pain it would cause them.

While I was at home, Stan returned. He held me as I cried more. He tried to get me to stay home for the rest of the day, but I insisted on going back to work. We prayed together.

I stared at myself in the bathroom mirror, trying to imagine that I had cancer. Then, I quickly reapplied my makeup and headed back to the office as if nothing was wrong.

Facing Reality

Imagine the façades of the people we come in contact with every day. I've heard the saying, "Every person you see looks better than they are"—and I think it's true. The people in our lives are walking around with real pain and hurt. I'm reminded of the compassion of Jesus and how He always had the time to stop, to notice people and their pain, and to help them.

Back in the office, I made my way to our human resources office. I told a dear friend and coworker I needed to talk to her. I wanted her to know I was sick and would be away from work.

"I have breast cancer."

I'll always remember her response. She gasped, putting her hand over her mouth. Then she started to cry. I remained calm, but her tears meant the world to me. She hugged me.

On the way home from work that day, I talked aloud to God. I stopped at the traffic light at the Vansant bridge. Around me, the autumn foliage in the mountains of southwest Virginia was breathtaking. I told God that just as He had the power to create the beauty in the color of the leaves, so He had power to remove this tumor. I'd seen miracles before, and I believed in His healing power. I claimed that God would perform a miracle in my life—and I would tell everyone about it.

Research, Research, Research

I didn't go to church that night but stayed home with my children. I didn't want them to be there when people found out I was sick.

When Stan came home, he was visibly shaken. He held me for a moment. Then I told him, "We can't eat or sleep. You get on one computer, and I'll get on the other. We have to learn as much as we can about this disease that has invaded my body." That night we also began to make a list of anyone we knew who might be able to help me. We began researching doctors and different hospitals. Stan began researching the type of cancer I had, using a copy of the pathology report provided by Dr. Sutherland.

I spoke with some friends who gave me valuable insight. A dear friend, Rebecca, mentioned MD Anderson Cancer Center in Houston, Texas. I didn't know anything about this hospital, but we wrote the name down on our research list.

That night Stan and I prayed and asked God to heal me. I felt His presence, although I was still scared. Images of cancer patients without hair raced through my mind, along with thoughts about the frightfulness of surgery, a breast prosthesis, and chemotherapy. It was all so overwhelming.

How did this happen to me? How did I catch this disease? I always thought I had good genes. Was it the water I was drinking, or the air I was breathing? *This cannot be happening!*

I thought about Sharon, who also worked at the bank. She too was the wife of a local pastor, and her cancer had metastasized to her liver and lungs. In fact, when her breast cancer spread, she came to me and we talked about her options. Back then, I didn't know a lot about cancer, and I wasn't sure I was any help to her. I'd watched her battle this disease for several years, and I thought about what was ahead for me.

The tornado of breast cancer swept through the bank, and two pastor's wives were caught in its web of pain and destruction. One lived. One died.

In loving memory of Sharon Kay Sparks Elkins—forty-two years well lived.

4

The Day After

Any child who grew up in the '80s can well remember the bomb drills that the elementary schools put us through. In the event of a nuclear attack, we were to get under our desks and put our heads between our knees. I wondered if this was just to help us get in a praying position, because otherwise it was worthless. During those days of the Cold War, I remember a movie called *The Day After*. It depicted the world the day after nuclear bombs were detonated. The frightening images were hard to get out of my mind.

And now I was confronted with another Day After.

On the day following my diagnosis, I awoke thinking about the conversation I'd had with God at the traffic light. I knew God could heal. My faith was strong. I'd committed my life, as had my husband, to leading others to put their faith in God.

I had confidence that morning that God had healed me during the night, and that I would be able to tell everyone of the power of God. I gathered my emotions and knew I had to check and see about the status of the tumor. I moved my hand across my chest—and the tumor was still there.

On my Day After, God said no.

Seasons Change

In the Bible, God tells us, "As long as the earth remains, there will be springtime and harvest, cold and heat, winter and summer, day and night" (Genesis 2:22, TLB).

As I looked outside, the seasons were changing. We'd had a great summer together as a family. The beach trip was just what we needed, and we spent valuable time together before school started. Now the autumn sky was bright, and the fall colors were a reminder of God's power. Yet I also knew that the cold, bitter winter was just around the corner.

In my body, I was also leaving summer and fall and headed for a dark, bitter, and cold winter. The pain was real. The fear was real. But spiritually—in a way that only God understands—I was going to leave winter and head into the promise of spring and summer. God was preparing me for a deeper relationship with Him, that could be achieved only through this trial in my life.

James, the half-brother of Jesus, wrote some powerful words to the church he was a part of in Jerusalem. The church was struggling, having been scattered around the known world and persecuted for their faith in Christ. James exhorted the believers to keep their faith and to stay strong. In his New Testament book, he mentions a series of tests that help us see if our faith is genuine. He begins with the test of trials. Through the Holy Spirit, James tells us that one of the ways we can measure whether our faith is genuine is by how we handle the trials of life: "Consider it pure joy, my brothers, whenever you face trials of many kinds, because you know that the testing of your faith develops perseverance" (James 1:2).

God was measuring the genuineness of my faith. I wondered how I would do.

The Calendar Turns

The day after the diagnosis, my phone rang all day. I didn't want to answer it. What do you say? Instead I stayed focus on learning about breast cancer and seeking out options.

I contacted a woman named Paula, who lived about two hours away and was a patient at MD Anderson Cancer Center in Houston. She talked with me a long time. She was honest about the difficulties of the disease, and she also praised the hospital and her surgeon there, Dr. R. I'll always be grateful for her help and for directing me to Dr. R.

On this day I realized the seriousness of my disease. I called the bank and said I wouldn't be back, and I didn't know how long I would be out. My coworkers were kind and understanding.

Two days later Stan and I traveled again to Kingsport, Tennessee, to see Dr. E., who had correctly diagnosed my cancer. We prayed that on this visit we could glean information as to the severity of my situation, and also get Dr. E.'s help for getting in to see Dr. R. at MD Anderson. We'd discovered that Dr. E. had actually worked at that hospital prior to coming to Kingsport.

Dr. E. was kind. He pulled out the pathology report and shared with me the details of what they found from the biopsy. The diagnosis was serious with multiple tumors, and it was feared that at least one tumor had grown into my chest wall.

I asked Dr. E. if he would get me an appointment with Dr. R. at MD Anderson. He told me he would try to help me get into the cancer center, but he didn't think he could get me in with Dr. R. I gave him the saddest look I could possibly muster up and said, "Please, try."

He left Stan and me in the little waiting room while he went to see what he could do.

If we live long enough, we all find ourselves in a waiting room, receiving bad news. It could be concerning our own health or that of another family member. It might be about the death of a spouse, or a child who has rebelled, or an aging parent in steep decline.

The waiting rooms of life are pivotal times that God can use to take us to a new place spiritually. The danger of the waiting room is that Satan also uses that time to tempt us with discouragement and bitterness.

I believe God protected me from such temptation by doing something miraculous in that waiting room, right after the worst news of my life had been confirmed. As we sat there nearly speechless, we were left with only two choices. We could either trust God, or we could deny Him.

God reminded us that day that He often does His best work when we're in the waiting room.

When Dr. E. returned to us, he responded, "Dr. R. is out of the country. He doesn't have an opening in his schedule for three weeks, and I don't even know if he would take you then as a patient."

My heart dropped with disappointment as I gazed over at Stan.

The doctor continued, "There's another doctor whose assistant I know, and I'll try to get you in with him."

He exited the room again, and Stan and I sat for an hour and a half waiting on a call from Houston. We prayed together, discussed the pathology information, and held onto hope.

At five o'clock, everyone in the office left except the doctor and his nurse. I stared at the clock watching each minute pass. Finally, the phone rang at 5:55. It was Dr. R.'s assistant. Dr. R. had unexpectedly called in from Mexico, and his assistant told him about my case. Dr. R. said he would see me the following Thursday at 11:00 a.m. (I already had appointments at Duke on Monday, Tuesday, and Wednesday. Thursday was the first day open in my calendar!)

At the traffic light in Vansant a few days earlier, I had prayed for God to instantly heal me. God chose to heal me in another way. Another miracle I prayed for—to get connected with Dr. R.—had just taken place, and I was amazed at how God spoke so clearly in the waiting room. I hugged the doctor and then the nurse. They seemed as excited as I was. Dr. E. quickly gave us information about flights and hotels in Houston.

At that moment, I knew God's hand was at work in my life.

A Life-Changing Dream

On Saturday night I dreamed of a verse I'd read in the Bible eight months earlier. As a busy mother of two little boys, a pastor's wife, and also working part-time at a bank, I can hardly remember what I did yesterday, much less recall a verse I'd casually read in my devotion time eight months earlier. In this dream, I was reading my Bible, and I kept reading the same verse over and over. I could see the words on the page so clearly.

I awoke at 4:00 a.m. As I sat up in bed, I began quoting the verse I'd been dreaming about—a verse I'd never memorized and only rarely read. I rolled out of bed and went into our living room, still quoting the words to myself over and over. Somehow I remembered that it was from the book of Habakkuk—a little Old Testament book that wasn't one I typically went to for encouragement and wisdom.

I turned on a lamp and opened my Bible to the third chapter of Habakkuk. It wasn't the verse I was looking for, but I was startled at the words I read: "I heard and my heart pounded, my lips quivered at the sound; decay crept into my bones, and my legs trembled. Yet I will wait patiently…"

No better description could be found for the moment I was told I had cancer. I thought, *I'm hallucinating—is this in the Bible?* I didn't remember ever reading that verse before.

I continued reading: "The Sovereign LORD is my strength; he

makes my feet like the feet of a deer, he enables me to go on the heights."

Then I turned to the first chapter in Habakkuk and found the verse that had awakened me from my sleep: "Look at the nations and watch—and be utterly amazed. For I am going to do something in your days that you would not believe, even if you were told."

I read the verse over and over. I sensed that God's Spirit was telling me, "I'm going to do something utterly amazing through your body. Now go and tell this to your congregation in the morning."

That encounter with God on October 23 would change the rest of my life.

Faces in the Crowd

I prayed and lay down in bed, but I never went back to sleep. I waited for Stan to wake up to get ready for Sunday morning worship. I wanted to share with him my encounter with God. I read to him the verses from Habakkuk. When I shared with him the sense that I needed to get up and share this at church, he encouraged me. He suggested I do it during the last point of his sermon. We prayed together, and I went to take my shower.

As I dried my hair, I thought, *I can't do this.* I just couldn't get up in front of everyone that morning. Since my diagnosis three days earlier, I'd sheltered myself here in our home. Just the thought of being in church and in a crowd of people made me anxious. *How will people react? Will they look at me funny? Will everyone feel sorry for me? Will people cry?* I dreaded that uncomfortable sorrow that everyone feels when they don't know what to say.

I walked out of the bathroom as Stan was preparing to leave for church and announced to him, "I can't do it." Emotionally, I just couldn't get up in front of all those people that day. I couldn't deal with it at this point. "I'm also really concerned about the kids," I told him. "We haven't talked to them yet about all that's happening. I'm afraid of people's reaction and what they might say that could scare them."

Stan put his arms around me and consoled me. He assured me it was okay not to do it. If I didn't feel comfortable speaking before everyone, that was fine. I had enough stress to deal with already.

My brother, Brian, had come to be with me for the weekend. We decided to leave the kids home with him and not take them to church. We felt that the best thing for them today was to shelter them from some of the harsh reality of my illness.

Brian and I had a casual, relaxed breakfast together. The boys were excited about having him there. While they were running around, I shared with Brian the verse I'd read from Habakkuk. I told him I felt I needed to go to church, but I didn't want to go. He told me to relax and not do anything that would add stress at this point.

I got dressed for church anyway. What would I wear? I rummaged through my closet, then my eyes rested on my favorite red dress. That's what I would wear. I applied some red lipstick, and decided, *I must go.*

I talked to God all the way to church. I asked Him to give me strength and help me know what to do. I arrived late and took a seat on the back pew.

As Stan gave the morning prayer requests, his voice broke, and he paused. My heart pounded, and I hurt for him. Stan isn't an outwardly emotional person, especially in the pulpit. Seeing him upset hurt me deeply. I knew he loved me, and that this diagnosis had been difficult for him.

As the congregation stood to sing, I decided to make my way to the front pew to sit beside Stan. He shouldn't have to bear this alone. And he shouldn't have to be the one to have to get up and discuss it.

As I began walking down the aisle, the fear and anxiety I'd felt that morning dissipated like the fog in the mountains. I knew everyone was looking at me, but that was okay. I went to the front pew, put my arm around Stan, and gave him a squeeze. I felt such a strong connection to him in that moment. How blessed I was to have a husband who loved me.

He glanced at me as if to say, "What do you want to do?"

I responded, "I want to do it."

After the singing, he made his way to the pulpit to deliver the morning message.

He got to his third point, and paused. "Now I want you to hear from one of the most courageous people I know—my wife."

As I made my way to the pulpit, it occurred to me that I had no idea what I was going to say, other than reading the verse from Habakkuk.

Although standing in front of a crowd was the last place I wanted to be that morning, I felt composed and at peace. I opened my Bible to Habakkuk. I calmly relived the events of the last twenty-four hours, then stated that I looked forward to reporting "utterly amazing" things to them in regard to my body.

I asked them to specifically pray for three things: safety in our travels; the ability to discern which hospital to go to for treatment; and that my children, Briggs and Glenn, would feel safe, secure, and unafraid.

I paused as I stated that last prayer request. A mental picture of the boys rushed through my mind, and I hurt in a place so deep in my heart that I didn't even know it existed until that moment.

As I returned to the front pew, I knew God had spoken through me, and I felt His Spirit in a powerful way.

5

Never Give Up

Growing up on a farm had an incredible impact on my life. The family farm was generational, first bought by my grandparents. My mother was raised on the farm, and, during my childhood, it was home for me, my parents, my brother, and for a time my grandmother, before she died. Our days there revolved around work and family. As a little girl, home was a place of comfort and safety.

I remember my pigtail phase. It was my hairstyle choice every day one summer. I can still remember the fun of riding on the back of the truck and feeling my pigtails blowing in the wind. I never mastered parting my hair straight and lining up my pigtails. My mother was always there to help. My brother, on the other hand, would sneak up behind me, pull on my pigtails, and yell, "Giddy up."

A few days after my diagnosis, I was leaving church when my hairdresser, Carmella, approached me. She told me she wanted to help me, and she knew I would need a wig. She said she would reschedule her appointments the next day to go with me to buy a wig and style it for me before I left for all my doctor's appointments out of town.

My mind raced. *A wig?* I was still believing in a miracle, and

I was praying my hair wouldn't fall out. After a few moments of denial, I knew she was right. We decided to leave early the next morning.

It was uncomfortable for me to step into a wig-and-prosthesis shop to purchase a wig. I kept telling myself to accept this and be strong. *It's just hair.*

By nature I'm conservative with money, but on this day I decided price was not a factor. I was going to purchase what made me feel good.

I couldn't have picked out a wig by myself; walking into the shop, I had no clue. But Carmella had already scoped the shop out the Saturday before, and knew a couple of good options for me. She'd been cutting and styling my hair for nine years.

She found one with the right color and length, and I tried it on, but it was just too poofy. She assured me she could thin it out and style it to look just like my current style. She also told me that a wig would fit and look different when you didn't have your own hair underneath it.

An essential item she brought that day was a camera. She took pictures of me in the wig both in the shop and outside in the natural light. Then she let me look at them. She was right. In the mirror it looked so fake, but outside in the natural light it looked much better.

We made the purchase, and I was set.

Striving for Control

Cancer is a disease that leaves you feeling helpless. As a young woman, I was used to taking charge and feeling some sense of control over my life. But cancer reminds you that any feeling of control is a façade. I felt healthy and looked healthy, yet my body was filled with cells that were sick and abnormal. And I had absolutely no control over what was happening.

Carmella prepared me: "When your hair begins to fall out, shave it. You have to take control." She also told me this would be a very emotional thing. She said every person whose head she'd shaved had cried while the clumps fell into their laps. She kept telling me how strong I'd been, and her words fueled my inner self.

I kept telling myself, "You can do this."

Carmella also told me to buy some self-tanner, because it would add color to my skin when I began to look washed out and sickly.

When faced with cancer, you need a good beauty-tip friend to help you deal with the unpleasant side effects of treatment. Carmella filled that role for me.

It Can't Touch Your Soul

My home growing up was not only a place of work and family, but it was also filled with N.C. State Wolfpack fans. In North Carolina, in a region often referred to as Tobacco Road, a person's college basketball allegiance is as unifying or divisive as anything else about him or her. You had to pick from Duke, North Carolina, or North Carolina State. At the farm that I called home, our allegiance tilted toward N.C. State.

One of the most memorable moments in college basketball history centered around N.C. State. The Wolfpack was playing the Houston Cougars for the 1983 NCAA championship. Houston, the top-rated team, was known as "Phi Slamma Jamma" because of how athletic and talented their starting lineup had proven to be during the season. N.C. State was a huge underdog.

The game was close and exciting. With just a few seconds remaining, N.C. State's guard Derrick Whittenberg threw up a long shot. It started to fall way short. But with only a second remaining, Lorenzo Charles grabbed the ball in midair before the basket and dunked it for the winning goal. N.C. State had won a national championship! State fans will always remember their head coach, Jim Valvano, running frantically around on the court afterward, trying to find someone to hug in his excitement of winning a national championship.

Just a few years after this incredible moment, Coach Valvano was diagnosed with cancer. During his battle with the disease, he appeared on ESPN's Espy Awards program on March 3, 1993, to receive the Arthur Ashe Courage & Humanitarian Award for his fight against cancer. That night Coach Valvano gave a memorable speech that included these remarks:

> Time is very precious to me. I don't know how much I have left....
>
> When people say to me, How do you get through life or each day, it's the same thing. To me, there are three things we all should do every day.... Number one is laugh. You should laugh every day. Number two is think. You should spend some time in thought. And number three is, you should have your emotions moved to tears—could be happiness or joy. But think about it. If you laugh, you think, and you cry, that's a full day....
>
> One last thing. I urge all of you, all of you, to enjoy your life, the precious moments you have. To spend each day with some laughter and some thought, to get your emotions going. To be enthusiastic every day and [as] Ralph Waldo Emerson said, "Nothing great could be accomplished without enthusiasm"—to keep your dreams alive in spite of problems whatever you have.

The ability to be able to work hard for your dreams to come true, to become a reality....

I said it before, and I'm gonna say it again: Cancer can take away all my physical ability. *It cannot touch my mind; it cannot touch my heart; and it cannot touch my soul.* And those three things are going to carry on forever.

Jim Valvano died April 28, 1993. The V Foundation for Cancer Research was established in his memory, and words he often spoke became its motto: "Don't give up...Don't ever give up."

6

Pivotal Decisions

It has been said that you make your decisions, and your decisions make you. Your life is the sum total of your decisions.

I was confronted with a decision that I believed could determine whether I lived or died. I believed my life was in the hands of God, and He is sovereign and good. However, at this point, I felt the stress of trying to discern His will in deciding which hospital to go to and which treatment option I should receive.

I faced three options.

One, I could go to MD Anderson in Houston. God had worked in utterly amazing ways to get me an appointment with Dr. R. Was that a sign from Him telling me that I was to receive treatment there?

Second, I could go to Duke University Medical Center in Durham. This option made more sense than Houston. The hospital was only a five-hour drive from Vansant—a long way, but much closer than Houston. The closer distance gave me better travel options and more opportunities to see my family. And I was more familiar with the hospital, since my dad had surgery several years earlier at Duke.

My third option was to stay at home and receive my treatments from a local doctor. I determined early on that this wasn't what God wanted me to do.

Often, when faced with a cancer diagnosis, you feel that something must be done immediately. You feel pressure, as if your tumor is growing inches every day, and if you don't have surgery or start chemotherapy immediately, your life will end.

While it's important not to delay crucial decisions, I've found in my experience that it's better to take a couple of days and do some research than to rush and make the wrong choice.

What was the right choice?

My first appointments were at Duke. Stan's parents had traveled from North Carolina to stay in Vansant with the kids as we went to Duke to explore what was available for me there. I can remember the nervousness and reluctance we felt as we loaded the car to make the five-hour drive.

While at the hospital that day, I realized I wasn't the only person fighting this horrible disease. As my journal reminds me, cancer does not discriminate.

October 26

Cancer—I don't know how this is possible.

Our day began with Stan saying a prayer. He prayed, "Today, we begin a journey of the unknown."

As we entered Duke Hospital I saw one sick person after another. I feel so good. What am I doing here?

An hour later, I passed out after a blood test and was being transported around the hospital in a wheelchair. Everything seemed so surreal.

I survived my first day of testing. God continues to place people in our lives. Some to encourage us, and others to help us. I pray for the pastor and his wife from South Carolina as he goes through pancreatic cancer. I pray for the couple from Virginia as she goes through chemo. I pray for God's healing of their bodies.

As the day comes to a close, I thank God for sending Donna (CAT scan tech) my way today, and for all her help in getting my film.

I realize that *peace* comes not by focusing on the mountain you have to climb, but on the *One* who can move the mountain.

We arrived at Duke Medical Center and wondered what the day would hold. We prayed the news would be better. I was scheduled to have a bone scan. I was frightened about the results of this test. There was a concern that at least one of the tumors had grown into my chest wall. If that had happened, the prognosis would be much different.

As I worried about all these tests, I wondered how different things could have been if my original doctor had been diligent and had reviewed my case more closely.

I hate the sight of needles and blood, especially if the needle's sticking in my body, and it's my blood I'm seeing. Stan had grown accustomed through the years of the effects of blood on me. So he wasn't surprised when I passed out during the very first test at Duke. Not a good start. I laugh at that now, knowing how many times I would be stuck, prodded, and probed during my cancer journey.

The doctors were informative and to the point. I was impressed with the oncologist and surgeon who examined me. There was further uncertainty concerning the growth of the tumor into my chest wall. Further tests were ordered. The bone and CAT scan were my main concerns at the moment. What if the cancer had spread to different areas of my body?

While I had my bone scan, Stan met a pastor from South Carolina. His cancer diagnosis was recent, and it had spread to his liver. He was in his thirties, just like Stan and me. Two pastors sat in that waiting room at Duke, one with cancer and the other there with his wife who had cancer. Both were young and serving God. The secret things really do belong to God.

Finally, some good news. The bone scan and CAT scan were clear. There were no visible signs of cancer in other areas of my body. We praised God and were thankful for this answered prayer.

We wrapped up our appointments at Duke later than expected. I was more impressed with Duke than Stan. He felt unsettled about the whole experience. This would be one of the first signs that God was leading us in a totally different direction.

Since we finished later than expected, we were in a frantic rush to get to Raleigh/Durham International Airport for an evening flight to Houston. My parents had driven down to Durham to be with me for my last day of testing at Duke. I'll never forget the look of concern on my dad's face as I hugged him and said goodbye. He was visibly shaken.

We arrived at the airport late and missed our flight. I cried and begged the airline employee to let us board—to no avail. I didn't imagine that my first major breakdown would be at the Raleigh/Durham airport. We spent the night in Raleigh, and God provided us with a flight to Houston early the next morning. It was going to be a challenge to get there on time for my first appointment.

October 28

Our day started at 3:30 a.m. We flew to Houston praying for a safe flight and the hope of a more encouraging diagnosis.

Susie Rife and her daughter, Traci, picked us up at the airport and quickly ushered us to MD Anderson Cancer Center. God continues to miraculously place people in our lives at the exact time that we need them.

The best part about today (and being tortured with tests is not a lot of fun) was the women I met. Some were points of encouragement for me while others were opportunities for me to share that you cannot go through a life-threatening disease without God. Everyone was interested in my story, and they were "utterly amazed" at how quickly I got into the hospitals.

Dr. R. ended our visit today with something I will always remember. He looked at me and said, "You're too nice of a person to be around not to make it." Then he came over and gave me the biggest hug and said, "You have every right to be optimistic."

The next day we met the oncologist we had been so kindly referred to by Dr. R. My first impression of Dr. T. was that of a great teacher. He taught me about the disease. He took out a legal pad and began writing down the particulars of my cancer. Then he discussed three different treatment options. One was standard treatment, the other two were clinical trials. I knew very little about clinical trials. My limited knowledge told me it was being the guinea pig to a new drug. Some patients would get the drug and some would not. Dr. T. taught us about the different phases of a clinical trial. He then discussed a trial that was in its third stage and showed us the results of the first two phases. It sounded very promising. Dr. R. had mentioned this same trial the day before.

Unfortunately, Dr. T. informed us that this particular trial was closed; they had accepted the last patient the evening before. We just missed it.

For a moment I felt like my chance of hope had fallen out of my pocket—kind of like the kid with the bell in *Polar Express*. How could I be so unlucky!

As I stared down at the legal pad, not having a clue which one of these treatment options would be best, I was disappointed that none were the same treatment path that had been recommended at Duke.

I looked up at Dr. T. and solemnly asked, "If I were your daughter, which one would you put her in?"

He paused, not wanting to answer the question. My eyes never wavered from his. He looked down and said, "I would put her in this one." He pointed to the description of the clinical trial that was closed.

I responded, "Then you *have* to get me in that trial." I was holding onto my thread of hope.

He answered, "I will."

I was reminded again of Habakkuk 1:5— "Look...watch...be utterly amazed."

The Agony of a Decision

We flew home from Houston just in time to spend Halloween with my two boys. On the day I had been diagnosed, I'd ordered Glenn a Batman costume and Briggs a baseball jersey. Normally I would have just found something inexpensive or borrowed something from a friend. This year I wanted the boys to have the costumes they desired.

But soon after our arrival home, it was apparent Halloween was not on Glenn's mind. He'd missed us deeply, and he wasn't about to hide his emotions or his need for attention from his parents. The magnificent Batman costume didn't see Halloween that year.

Looking into their eyes, I prayed that this wouldn't be the last Halloween we spent together.

The decisions were weighing on me. Where would we go? Which hospital's treatment would work? How would we afford this? Who would care for my children? Although I felt peace and hope at Houston—how would we do it? The logistics of that arrangement seemed far greater than my mind could conceive. Duke was closer to home, and familiar. My family would be close to help.

Stan and I prayed for God to give us wisdom. We asked our church, family, and friends to pray for our decision.

The analytical side of my brain said, "One of these treatment options is superior." "Not all roads will lead you to the same destination." "You must choose the correct path."

For the next three days I didn't sleep. I researched. I sent my pathology report to Johns Hopkins Hospital in Baltimore, Maryland, for a third opinion, hoping that someone would concur to the treatment path I should follow. Their quick reply only muddied the water—still another treatment option that was different from the first two hospitals. How could this be?

I began to speak with other doctors and made contact with an oncologist at University of Virginia. I spoke with an individual who did cancer research in Washington state about the various drugs used in the different treatment plans. I faxed each of them my pathology report. Also, I called a childhood friend who is a radiologist to see if she had any insight. I spoke to numerous cancer survivors.

I felt like my quantity of life depended on this one decision. I looked at my boys and felt overwhelmed with responsibility. What if I went down the wrong road? How would I live with that? What would I tell my children? "Mommy chose the wrong medicine."

Panicked, I decided to straddle the fence. It was Monday, and I had another appointment at Duke on Wednesday, with chemo scheduled to begin on Thursday. I also had an appointment at MD Anderson on Thursday.

As the clock that night struck 11:00, I had no idea where I would be in two days.

Discovering Mistakes

I sat in my blue chair in the living room reading my Bible. I've always believed that God speaks to His people. How close He had seemed during the past twelve days! I prayed that God would help me shut out the outside world, and people's opinions and suggestions. I knew God would speak to us through His Word. I asked Him to please show me in a profound, mighty way which road to take.

Again and again I went over the reports and information I'd gathered. I kept seeing the drug Herceptin mentioned. I'd never heard of it. Preliminary research appeared very promising for this drug given to women who were HER2/neu positive—the club of which I was a part. Why hadn't Duke included this in my regimen? I pondered this all night.

The next morning I tried to reach my doctor at Duke, but she was unavailable. I kept calling until they finally let me speak with the doctor's physician assistant (PA). We begin going over my diagnosis and recommended treatment. When I questioned the drugs prescribed, she stated, "You are HER2/neu negative."

"No," I responded. "I'm HER2/neu positive."

"I'm looking at your chart in front of me," the PA said, "and you're HER2/neu negative."

"I'm looking at my original pathology report," I replied, "and I'm HER2/neu *positive.*"

Being a banker, I had no medical knowledge. For a moment I thought, *Am I reading this wrong? Maybe I've lost too much sleep.*

There was a pause before the PA said, "I'm sorry, but your chart is incorrect. Whoever filled out your chart marked you as HER2/neu negative. You're right—you're HER2/neu positive. When you meet with the doctor tomorrow, she'll give you a new regimen."

Part of me freaked. Was someone trying to kill me? How could I be the recipient of so many medical mistakes? What if I hadn't caught that? What if I had six months of chemo, all the while taking the wrong drugs?

Chemo Prep

That same day, I hurried to the nail salon. A dear friend had given me her nail appointment. I love having my nails done, but I pamper myself with this luxury only once a year. As I prepared for chemo, the doctors discussed having healthy nails and the side effect of sometimes losing your nails. I was advised not to cut my nails once I began chemo, but only to file them. This trip to the nail salon was my attempt to have my nails short and healthy before the injection of poison in my veins that would kill the cancer cells.

I walked into the salon wanting a moment of relaxation, but small-town beauty shops and nail salons can be quite a gathering place and gossip scene. (Does *Steel Magnolias* ring a bell?) I walked in and instantly felt everyone's eyes looking at me. It was the same experience I'd had every time I'd entered a public place since the day I was diagnosed. "There's Susan, the young preacher's wife with small children who has breast cancer." They looked at you as if you'd been given a death sentence and would surely never live. I felt uncomfortable. How was I to act? Sad? Stressed? Not worried?

To make matters worse, everyone felt compelled to tell you a story—some about survivors, others about individuals who fought a good fight but their life ended prematurely. It was all so awkward.

I'd known Beth for many years. I sat down in her pedicure chair, and she remarked, "Susan, I hear you're doing well, but everybody who comes in here says Stan is a wreck."

I didn't know how to respond to this. My heart ached. I realized that while Stan appeared strong around me, his anguish was apparent to his church family and friends. I lifted up a prayer, *God bless Stan.*

Then I quickly told her what I wanted. "Clean and trim my nails and toenails. No polish, but possibly some nail hardener."

Beth had treated lots of cancer patients and knew just what to do. She even gave me some cuticle oil and instructed me to use it daily.

She began to work on my feet, and in her transparent demeanor she asked, "So, are you going to Texas?"

I responded, "I don't know."

"What? I heard about how you miraculously got in to see that doctor. That must be God working."

I listened.

Feeling the need to justify all my decisions, I added that this issue was complicated and I wasn't sure which treatment option to take, or if doing a clinical trial was the best decision.

She continued to work while sharing stories of other cancer patients she'd had as customers.

Then two other ladies I knew walked in, one a former coworker and the other a friend I went to church with. They shared how they'd been praying for me. I begin to share how God had been working in my life, how divine intervention has directed me. I mentioned my indecision about where to receive treatment.

Inwardly I began to digest the phone conversation I'd had with the PA just moments before I arrived at the salon. As I told Beth about this conversation, she stopped her work and looked up at me. "Susan," she said, "God's calling you to Texas."

At that moment I knew she was right.

I just didn't want to go.

Your Decisions Make You

I came home and put my children to bed. I lay in Glenn's bed with Briggs on one side and Glenn on the other. I read them a book. We said a prayer together. The boys both prayed, "Dear Jesus, help Mommy's boo-boos to get better." Tears streamed down my face, but I made sure neither child saw them.

I prayed, "God, thank You for Briggs, Glenn, Daddy, and our family. Thank You that You love us and that You're always with us, no matter where we are." I kissed their faces and put my arms around them both until they drifted off to sleep.

My eyes circled the room. I could hear the Thomas-the-Train clock ticking. I wished I could stay right there between them forever.

Slowly, I got up. Pausing in the doorway, I stared a few minutes longer at the peacefulness of their sleep. *God be with them. Protect them. May Your love surround them. May they fear not.*

You make your decisions, and your decisions make you.

Later, I would discover that the oncologist I'd seen at Duke was pregnant. Therefore, her maternity leave would have coincided with my treatment time there, had I gone to Duke.

God is sovereign, and He is good.

I packed my bags for Houston.

7

Houston, We Have a Problem

*We humans make plans,
but the LORD has the final word.*

PROVERBS 16:1, TLB

As I made my way down the hallway to our den, Stan was at his laptop making flight arrangements for the next day. We planned to fly down to Houston where I would receive a chemo treatment, then fly home a week later. My parents would come to Vansant and stay with the boys. It would be good for them to spend time with their grandparents. This would be the longest my dad had ever stayed with the kids. All would be well. The plans were made, and the plans were good.

It was midnight, and I was still doing laundry and trying to decide what to pack. I would need to take my wig, my Bible, some uplifting music, and comfortable clothes. I packed my suitcase for the week-long trip, just as planned.

Plans. We've all made them, and the level of our dysfunction determines how many plans we have and how closely to the plans we feel we must adhere.

For instance, Stan and I are polar opposites when it comes to planning a vacation. Stan's idea of vacation planning is to decide which week it will be. That's the extent of it. When that week comes, he's ready to go—some place, somewhere—to do whatever there is to do when you get there, while you stay wherever you can find to stay along the way.

On the other hand, there's my way of planning a vacation. You pick the week, and you collect all the information available about the destination spot. You study the material like you're on a sacred journey. After hours of preparation and fact finding, it's time to map out the schedule for the vacation. There cannot be a single wasted moment. Every day must be filled with educational, recreational, family-building, and memory-lasting activities so that every penny spent on this trip will be used the most effective way. There can be no wasted time. You can always rest and relax the next week, when you're back in the routine of home and work.

The Best-Laid Plans

The funny thing about our plans is that they're often different from God's plans. "If you want to make God laugh," someone has said, "tell Him your plans." I've surely brought laughter to heaven, because I told God my mapped-out plans for how this cancer journey was going to go.

Shannon Stone was someone else who had a plan. This Texas firefighter and father of six-year-old Cooper was a committed Texas Rangers baseball fan. He was excited when he won a lottery drawing for tickets to the 2010 World Series between the Rangers and the San Francisco Giants. And though the Rangers lost that series, Stone was looking forward to 2011.

He had a great plan. He took Cooper to Arlington Stadium to

see the Rangers play. It would be a father-and-son night, doing what previous generations of fathers and sons have done. It was at the end of the fifth inning when the plans Shannon made changed. Conor Jackson of the Oakland Athletics hit a foul ball close to outfielder Josh Hamilton, the star player for the Texas Rangers. Hamilton caught the foul ball and did what he'd done many times. He threw the ball into the stands for a fan to have and enjoy as a souvenir.

Jeff Passan of Yahoo! Sports described what happened next:

> Hamilton's toss came in short. It didn't stop Shannon Stone from stretching to grab it. I'm almost certain, in fact, that the moment before Shannon Stone fell 20 feet and suffered injuries that would kill him, he was indescribably happy. He was going to grab a baseball from Josh Hamilton, a man who hauled himself from the depths of drug addiction to not only return to baseball but win the American League MVP award last season. Once Stone had that baseball, he was going to hand it to his son. And for the rest of his life, his son would have a story to tell about the time his daddy reached over a railing and snagged a bad throw from Josh Hamilton, one of the most talented players ever to wear a baseball uniform.
>
> Instead, he watched his dad die. He saw Shannon Stone secure the ball in both hands but lose his balance in the process. The man next to Stone reached, in vain, to grab his leg. Stone fell head first 20 feet. When paramedics arrived to stabilize Stone and take him to a hospital, the relief pitchers in the A's bullpen overheard the conversation.
>
> "Please check on my son," Stone said.

He died later at a local hospital.

When we make our plans, we're always thinking about the best. Surveys are always coming out that tell us the best of everything—the best places to raise kids, or to vacation, or to retire, or to own a home—the list goes on. But what happens when the best doesn't happen?

God's desire for His people is that we feel secure in His love and power. Everything else in life might be unstable—our health, our family, our education, and our world. Everything else is uncertain. But God has a plan.

God, the Ultimate Planner

In the Old Testament, we often find the people of God in trouble. At one point, because of His people's persistent disobedience, God allowed King Nebuchadnezzar of Babylon to attack Jerusalem and take a number of people into captivity. This tragedy, six centuries before Christ, was the first of several deportations of the Jewish people. The young men Daniel, Shadrach, Meshach, and Abednego were part of this deportation.

During this time, God instructed His prophet, Jeremiah, to write a letter to these Jewish captives in Babylon:

> This is what the LORD Almighty, the God of Israel, says to all those I carried into exile from Jerusalem to Babylon: "Build houses and settle down; plant gardens and eat what they produce. Marry and have sons and daughters; find wives for your sons and give your daughters in marriage, so that they too may have sons and daughters. Increase in number there; do not decrease. Also, seek the peace and prosperity of the city to which I have carried you into exile. Pray to the

LORD for it, because if it prospers, you too will prosper." Yes, this is what the LORD Almighty, the God of Israel, says: "Do not let the prophets and diviners among you deceive you. Do not listen to the dreams you encourage them to have. They are prophesying lies to you in my name. I have not sent them," declares the LORD.

This is what the LORD says: "When seventy years are completed for Babylon, I will come to you and fulfill my good promise to bring you back to this place." (Jeremiah 29:4–10)

God tells His people, "You might as well get used to it—you're going to be there for a while! So go ahead, build homes, plant gardens, get married, have children—because you'll be in Babylon for seventy years."

Such news from God doesn't seem very kind or merciful. Seventy years! They had hoped this would be a short detour in their lives; now many of them learned they would be spending the rest of their lives in captivity. Certainly, this couldn't be the plan.

As God continues speaking through Jeremiah, he offers this encouragement:

"For I know the plans I have for you," declares the LORD, "plans to prosper you and not to harm you, plans to give you hope and a future. Then you will call upon me and come and pray to me, and I will listen to you. You will seek me and find me when you seek me with all your heart. I will be found by you," declares the LORD, "and will bring you back from captivity. I will gather you from all the nations and places where I have banished you," declares the LORD, "and will bring you back to the place from which I carried you into exile." (Jeremiah 29:11–14)

In 538 B.C., Persia's army conquered Babylon. Two years later, Cyrus, the Persian king, allowed the Jews to return home to Israel— exactly seventy years after they were taken into captivity. Even in their captivity, God did not forget His people. He had a plan. There in the middle of the book of Jeremiah, we find Him telling His captive people, "I know the plans I have for you."

For me, it seemed like I was being held captive by cancer and by all the decisions I was being forced to make. Yet the truth is that even in my captivity, God had a plan. As Corrie ten Boom (a Dutch Christian who saved many Jews during World War II) said, "Never be afraid to trust an unknown future to a known God."

It's utterly amazing how God had a plan for my life, even though I didn't like the plan when He revealed it to me. Though I didn't realize it, God was orchestrating His plan from the beginning of this trip to Houston.

November 3

Glen and Pauline took us to the airport.... On the way to the airport, Pauline said something to me I will never forget. I was talking to her about all the research and different doctors I had talked to, and she replied, "You've been talking to the doctors while we've been talking to Jesus."

How powerful!

Finally we arrived at Houston. I tried to settle down in our room. Before drifting off to sleep, I prayed, "God, perform a miracle in my life. God heal me." I quoted to myself the verses from Habakkuk.

November 4

Today was a difficult day. We had our second visit with Dr. T. about my treatment. Two things he told me were difficult to accept.

First, I will have a central venous catheter (CVC) placed below my collarbone to deliver my chemo.

Second, he said I could not go home for a *month*, and he would only allow me to do that if things were going well.

I instantly became numb. I took no more notes and asked no more questions. My response back was, "I can't do that. I can't be away from my kids."

His response back to me: "You only have one chance to beat this." He walked to the door and began to turn the handle, then quickly turned around and looked me in the eyes and said, "One day your boys will thank me." Then, he left the room.

I left the doctor's office thinking, "I'm not going to do this." I want to go back to Duke.

As I walked to the hotel room, tears filled my eyes. There is nothing they can do to me physically that hurts as deeply as being separated from my children.

Then I remembered that God loves Briggs and Glenn more than I do, and He loves *me* that much too!

❦

After the long day with the doctors, and God revealing a different plan than what I had mapped out, Stan and I spent a quiet evening together. Neither of us had much to say. Sometimes stillness and quietness is best.

We were staying at the Rotary House, an extraordinary hotel designed for MD Anderson patients. It's actually attached to the hospital, providing the comforts of a hotel room while having immediate access to hospital care. It's a wonderful concept for a cancer center.

That evening we relished talking with the boys by phone. They brought us both so much joy. Small, simple things brought excitement to them, even during such a scary time of separation. We told them we could see the Texans football field from our room, and they were so excited and wanted us to take a picture for them. They seemed to be having a wonderful time with their grandparents.

Sitting in my room watching TV, a news flash announced that Elizabeth Edwards, wife of vice-presidential candidate John Edwards, had breast cancer. I was shocked and saddened for her, and instantly felt a connection with a woman I didn't even know. I wondered where she would receive treatments. I knew that with her financial and political influence, she was likely to receive the best treatment available.

I watched her announcement over and over on TV as the networks replayed it. Her cancer diagnosis was the story of the day. I wondered if breast cancer was rising in young women. Or was I just more aware since my own diagnosis? I looked at pictures of Elizabeth Edwards with her children, and I was heartbroken for them.

It was late, and I sat on my bed focusing on the picture of my own children taken at the beach, a picture I looked at every day. The boys' sweet faces.

I prayed for Elizabeth Edwards and her children.

Sleep was minimal that night. I was so nervous, my mind would not rest.

8

Sticky Notes and the Voice of God

Arthur Fry sang in a church choir and struggled to keep his bookmarks in place in his hymnal. He wanted a marker that wouldn't shift and fall out, but that could also be easily removed.

One of Fry's coworkers at the 3M Company was a man named Spencer Silver, who worked in the firm's research laboratories trying to find new and better adhesives. One of the products Silver developed was a weak adhesive that stuck to objects, but could easily be lifted off. It was super weak instead of super strong, and no one at 3M had figured out a marketable use for it.

Arthur Fry took some of this seemingly worthless adhesive and coated the back of his paper bookmarks for use in his hymnal. And thus, the sticky note was invented.

The sticky note was almost an accident. Yet it's one of the most used inventions in modern times. Think about how often you use a sticky note. It has been life changing!

God, in His sovereign power, used a sticky note to speak to me in a powerful way at one of the scariest moments of my life.

November 5

Today I had a central venous catheter placed in my chest. I dreaded this procedure and was nervous about them puncturing my lung.

When the nurse took my blood pressure and heart rate, my heart rate was elevated. She asked me if I wanted her to call my doctor to give me something to relax. I said no. I began to take deep breaths, trying to relax. Then I had a mental conversation with myself. "Be calm. Relax. Practice your Lamaze breathing. God, help me."

Then I noticed a small sticky note on the adjacent wall. It read, "Psalm 103: Praise the Lord. O my soul; all my inmost being, praise his holy name. Praise the Lord, O my soul, and forget not all his benefits—who forgives all your sins and heals all your diseases."

I didn't have my glasses on, yet for a moment I was able to focus and read that scripture.

Utterly amazing!

Comfort and Cure

We tried to make our first weekend in Houston enjoyable, knowing I would start chemo on Monday. I had no idea what that would be like. Meanwhile, the separation from the boys was difficult on all of us.

Our friend, Traci, took us shopping on Saturday. I decided to phone the boys and ask what they would like me to send them. I yearned to hear joy in their voices and think of sparkles in their eyes.

I was determined to get them both something they wanted.

Briggs wanted a University of Texas jersey and helmet. For once in his life, he could consider it done. Then Glenn got on the phone. "Mommy, bring me a baby."

Dead silence. I gasped, "Bring you what?"

"A baby."

That was definitely not the response I expected. Glenn had never before mentioned wanting a baby in our family. Where had this come from?

I began one of those parent/child conversations, trying to explain to a three year old that I couldn't bring him a baby.

He responded, "Aren't you at the hospital?"

Then the lightbulb clicked on. The only time Glenn knew of anyone's mommy going to the hospital was to have a baby. Smart kid! Aren't mommies supposed to bring you babies from the hospital?

I ended the conversation assuring Glenn that I would send him something special he could play with.

I got off the phone and wanted to burst into tears. My mind told me to laugh instead.

The conversation with Glenn reminded me of what Monday would bring. Chemo would put my body into menopause. The doctors had discussed this with Stan and me. They discussed the option to harvest and store my egg cells. We decided against it. Stan and I had discussed having another child many times throughout the years. We had decided to put it on hold until Stan finished the coursework for his doctor of ministry degree. Cancer had ended all that. After four years of diligent work and studies, Stan dropped out of the doctoral program a week after my diagnosis. He was almost finished. All the time and money. The dreams. Why?

I concluded it wasn't God's will for me to have another child. As for Stan's degree, I wondered if he would ever get the opportunity to finish. I felt guilty that my illness was causing so many people pain.

That Saturday morning, I distracted my mind and emotions with retail therapy. A sports store. I purchased a helmet and jersey set for each of the boys—University of Texas Longhorns for Briggs and Green Bay Packers for Glenn. I closed my eyes and imagined them running around the house pretending to be football stars—sweet thoughts for my mind and my soul.

That evening, we ended the day with Texas barbecue.

The next morning we had the privilege of going to Second Baptist Church of Houston. We met several people. Each was kind and offered to help in any way possible. I knew God's love through His church abounded everywhere.

The sermon that morning was from the third chapter of Romans. The pastor's points were interesting:

1. Face the seriousness of the diagnosis.
2. Be ready for the cure.
3. Celebrate the wonder of the cure.

I wanted to stand up in the middle of the service and say, "Did you write this just for *me*?" Then I felt the Holy Spirit saying, "Of course I wrote this for you. I know the appointed time and place that you will be, and I love you enough to send a sermon to the pastor of the third largest church in the United States just for you."

As I left the sanctuary, I again had that feeling that I was on an unusual journey and didn't know where it was taking me. I felt renewed strength and courage to continue putting one foot in front of the other.

Photographs and Fears

Traci took a picture of Stan and me before we left the church. I wanted to remember what I looked like and who I was before the chemo treatments began. Deep down in my soul, I felt I would never be the same.

Sunday afternoon we relaxed on the patio outside the Rotary House, enjoying the beautiful fall day. My mind raced with questions that would be answered only through personal experience: What does chemo feel like? Can you feel it going through your veins? Would I get sick instantly? Would I spend the whole night throwing up?

I hate throwing up. As a child I had throw-up phobia. I could count on one hand the number of times I'd thrown up until my first pregnancy. I was always the one who in a time of nausea would lie perfectly still for fear that one tiny movement might bring on the revolting of my digestive tract. I could never understand those people who actually stuck their fingers down their throat so they would throw up and feel better. I'm not sure which would rank as worse—the fear of throwing up or the fear of needles. The next day I would start chemotherapy—which involved both.

I've always heard that our experiences in life prepare us for something later on. I had battled morning sickness through both of my pregnancies. When I was pregnant the second time, and Briggs was eighteen months old and not yet toilet-trained, I remember him walking into a bathroom and gagging into the toilet. Obviously he'd watched his mother do it enough times that he thought this was what you were supposed to do in a toilet.

I consoled myself that at least I could handle throwing up better now than ten years ago. Focus on the bright side of things.

Twenty-four Hours

As we relaxed that Sunday afternoon, I looked over at Stan, who seemed content reading a book and taking time for a nap or two on the chaise longue. I could hear children playing outside, and my mind filled with images of Briggs and Glenn.

If being separated from my children wasn't gut-wrenching enough, the further information that had been provided by Dr. T. on Friday was. He'd told us that not only would I have treatments every week, but my chemo would last for twenty-four hours straight. That's right—an entire twenty-four-hour infusion of poison into my veins. Although this is no longer an uncommon treatment, at the time I'd never heard of someone taking chemo for that long—even though, being in the ministry, I spent time with a lot of sick people.

I hated the response I received from everyone back home when I told them. There was always a pause, then the inquiring "Really?" Followed by, "I've never known anyone to take chemo for twenty-four hours." I would hear statements like, "Mama's treatments took about two hours, and she was so sick." Thanks for the encouragement.

Slowly those Sunday evening hours passed for Stan and me, and then it was 10:00 p.m. Time for bed.

Then it was Monday morning.

November 8

I start my first chemo treatment.

❧

As we walked to the infusion therapy area, this thought kept racing through my head: *O God, help me not be a wimp. At least not on the outside.*

I took a deep breath and opened the door. As I walked in, I carefully canvassed the infusion therapy room. I was obviously the only patient with hair. I picked up a magazine and waited with everyone else to have my name called. I had my eyes half-cocked as I carefully examined each one in the room. Some were in wheelchairs. Most wore caps over their heads. One nicely dressed middle-aged woman wore an obvious wig. A guy who looked to be younger than me was completely bald—add a lollipop and he could be Kojak, except his color was terrible. He appeared to be accompanied by his mother. He was tall and very thin, but jaunty. I wondered what was wrong with him.

I don't belong here, I told myself. *These people are sick.* I ran my hands through my shoulder-length hair. Then my eyes met those of another patient across the room, and I was embarrassed. Her look told me she wondered what I was doing here. I felt guilty for having hair, and wondered if I would look like her.

It was similar to the feeling you get when you go to the OB doctor for the first time after finding out you're pregnant. You see those women nine months pregnant in the waiting room, and you think, *I'll never look like that.*

"Susan Parris?"

I swallowed a knot, and Stan and I rose to meet the nurse at the front of the room. She quickly checked my arm bracelet and asked for my patient number. Then she ushered us back into a room that was very small and private. There was a chair for a caretaker and a TV mounted to the wall.

She carefully explained the procedure. She discussed how some patients have allergic reactions to Taxol. My first treatment would begin with a very slow infusion. "If you feel faint or dizzy, or you start breaking out in a rash, or have any unusual symptoms, please let us know immediately." I thought, *I feel all of those, and I haven't even been hooked up to anything yet!*

It began with premeds through an IV hooked to the CVC line

in my chest and then the chemo began. I felt it going through my veins. It's a cold sensation. They brought in warm blankets and wrapped me up. I tried to focus on the TV, and Stan held my hand. I began to feel extremely sleepy. As hard as I tried, I couldn't stay awake. I drifted off.

After twelve hours, they determined it would be okay for me to go back to my room at the Rotary House.

They packed the remaining twelve hours of my chemo fluids into a briefcase-type bag, still attached to the CVC line. I carried it with me back to our room.

Twelve hours later the process was over.

November 9

I finished my first chemo treatment.

The pattern for my treatments would stay basically the same. Stan spent the whole day in a tiny room with me. The staff brought him a tray from the cafeteria so that he never left my side.

I felt some nausea, but continued to take the anti-nausea medicine. For the most part I felt okay. I became overly paranoid about symptoms that I thought were normal. As I washed my hair, I wondered if any would fall out. It didn't. I felt relieved, at least for the moment.

The doctor informed us that my blood counts would be their lowest about ten days after this first treatment, and to be careful about crowds.

It was Wednesday, and a beautiful sunny day in Houston.

9

Not One Bad Cell

As Stan and I visited a history museum exhibit about the Dead Sea Scrolls in Houston, I discovered how my faith looks both backward and forward. It's amazing how these scrolls were preserved for more than 2,000 years. I saw a scroll of Habakkuk from the second century and didn't realize how much it reflected my future.

Once again I could feel the presence of God all around me.

November 10

Tonight, Stan and I went to church here in Houston. We paid $40 for a taxi to take us to and from church. I didn't know going to church could be so expensive. But I knew when I got there it was meant to be, and worth far more than $40.

The sermon was on Habakkuk. Utterly amazing! I was convicted of how many times in our ministry we have failed to wait on God. Stan and I have wanted to take control and move God along in the process. No more—I want to wait for His miraculous timing.

Thank You, God, for Habakkuk and for speaking to me with Your still quiet voice. Thank You for the lady who prayed for me, "Not one bad cell in her body!"

As long as I live, I'll never forget my experience at church that Wednesday evening. In my thirty-four years, I couldn't recall hearing a sermon preached on Habakkuk. When I picked up the sermon outline and saw where the text was from, I felt chills all over.

I knew God was right beside me. Of the thousands of people in this auditorium, God had meant this message and this night for *me*. The orchestration of these events was humbling to me, but mostly powerful. How quickly we forget the power of God! *O Lord,* I prayed, *I don't care if I live or die, I just want to experience Your power while I have breath.*

During the prayer time, I felt the Holy Spirit moving in my life, and I went up front to have someone pray with me. It was a small-frame, African-American, middle-aged woman. Even the touch of her hand was calming. I told her I had cancer. She prayed the most beautiful prayer. The words of her last sentence will always echo in my mind: "Lord, may not one bad cell be found in her body."

Ups and Downs

On Friday, Stan left for Virginia. He was going home to see and reassure the boys and to preach on Sunday.

Two of my friends flew in to stay with me for the weekend. I'm so grateful for the sacrifice they made. I was still battling nausea and some pain.

November 12

This has been my week: Felt great… sick… felt good… sick… felt good… pain… felt good… pain. Get the picture?

It reminded me of when I was a child and would ride the seesaw with Brian at the Lake Junaluska playground. One minute you are up, the next you are down. So it seems to be the state of this journey I am currently on.

The best thing about a seesaw is the only way you stay down is if you want to. With determination and a push of your feet you can always get back up. Being on top has always been my favorite place to be, even if I don't get to stay for very long!

Thanks to all my prayer partners for lifting me to the top with the weight of your prayers!

They discovered today that the catheter in my chest is infected. Stan had already left to go back to Virginia. I was by myself and started getting sick while they were treating it. The nurse attending me took such good care, and I told her that God had placed her in my path today. She asked me if I was a Christian, and I said yes. She then closed the door took my hands and prayed the most beautiful prayer.

We are never alone, and I continue to be utterly amazed at the works of God. The prayers of righteous men and women availeth much!

Susie and Carmella arrived later in the evening, and I was so glad to see them. They were a remembrance of home, the love of my church family. Carmella was my hairdresser, and I needed all the beauty tips I could get. Our goal was to cut my hair. I'd originally planned for her to shave my head, but I'd heard of some cancer patients *not* losing their hair. My oncologist had assured me that mine *would* come out, but after five days, there was still no sign of that. So I decided on just a short cut. In my thirty-four years of life, I'd *never* had short hair.

In the process of taking my shoulder-length hair to a short cut, we decided to show a few different styles in between—to get creative and have fun! We had lots of fun despite my nausea and bouts of throwing up. For the most part I felt cruddy, and the question trickled often across my mind: *How would I make it for twenty-four weeks of this?*

Since I threw up all over the bathroom at the first restaurant and almost fainted at the second, we decided to order room service and stay in the room the rest of the weekend. The girls came prepared with lots of great magazines. We flipped through them and talked about decorating our homes. I shared how I'd been wanting to paint my bedroom. I thought celery would be a good color. We laughed, talked about our husbands, and offered a few confessions. Normal girl time stuff.

Sunday afternoon I was already dreading their departure early Monday morning. They represented my old life—before cancer had invaded.

The Rotary House was expensive, as was all the travel back and forth—not to mention how much our part of the medical coinsurance would be. I wondered how Stan and I were going to pay for all of it. As those thoughts circulated in my mind, the girls shared with me about a lady in our community who felt like God was leading her to help me. She'd given a gift of $5,000 to help with our medical expenses. I was shocked, and touched. I felt the arms of God wrap around me. It would be the beginning of an outpouring of love and financial assistance that would sustain us.

I couldn't sleep. The medication kept me awake all night, and 4:30 a.m. came quickly.

As the girls left, I cried and gave them a little gift I'd picked up in the hotel gift shop. It was a painted metal sleigh-bell ornament with the word *Joy* printed on it. I thought of my childhood Sunday school teacher telling us that *joy* stands for Jesus, Others, and You. They had certainly displayed that by coming to stay with me for the weekend.

Round Two

It wouldn't be long before it was time for me to start my next chemo treatment. As the morning unfolded, I felt worse and worse, to the point I didn't think I could get out of the bed. My whole body just felt so strange. I was nauseated and felt like I would faint. I was tired but couldn't sleep. When I opened my eyes, I felt dizzy.

November 15

Today was a difficult day. I was by myself and very sick. It's so strange how things can change in a week. Last week I went to my first chemo treatment feeling great but scared. Today I was taken in a wheelchair because I was too sick to walk. I even got sick on my way from the room to the hospital, throwing up all over the floor. I could have died. The young guy who was pushing me was so nice. I was so embarrassed! I told him I was sorry and he told me he was sorry I was sick. God never fails to place angels in our path.

I lost four pounds in three days—not good for a thin-structured woman. However, just when you think it can't get any worse, *it doesn't*. They gave me some fluids through an IV and some new anti-nausea medicine. I was able to take my treatment.

Two down and twenty-two to go!

Tonight I am feeling much better. Stan is back, and I am so blessed to have such a wonderful and loving husband.

Once again, prayers have lifted me to the top of the seesaw!

What I'd learned in this first week of chemo was that when you feel sick, tell someone. Don't try to keep toughing it out. Once they changed my anti-nausea medication and I quit taking the pain medicine, I felt better. This lesson applies to life as well. We often hold in our thoughts and struggles because we don't want to burden others, but we can't be blessed by what change might be offered to us.

November 17

Today has been a mental game for me. I am trying to figure out how we are going to manage with me in Houston and my children in Virginia. How is this feasible? We have made it work for a few weeks but reality has set in. I am just living day by day, week by week—a stark contrast from how I prefer to navigate my life.

I don't know how Stan can keep flying back and forth, taking care of me, the kids, and his job! Aside from the finances—and that is huge—the logistics are just more than my mind can figure out today.

As Stan and I discuss this, we get an email from dear friends, David and Rebecca. How timely. They have sent us an email outlining all the different doable options we should consider. Totally out-of-the-box thinking! Most people ask us the obvious question, "How are you going to do this?" Adding stress to my already stressed self! Not David. He has an analytical mind and is a great problem solver as well as a trusted friend. He and Rebecca list for us six possibilities for making this journey work.

I remember my son's Sunday school verse that was posted to our refrigerator the day I left for Houston: "With God all things all possible" (Matthew 19:26).

Dramatic Change

It was the tenth day after my first chemo. I knew my counts should be getting low, but I felt great. I had a scheduled appointment with Dr. T.

November 18

Praise God from whom all blessings flow,
Praise Him all creatures here below,
Praise Him above ye heav'nly host,

Praise Father, Son, and Holy Ghost.

Amen.

These were the first words that came to mind today as we met with the doctor. This was one of the first hymns that I learned as a child. We sang it in church every Sunday. Today, it rings so true in my life.

God answered our prayers today. The doctor examined me and they were "utterly amazed" at what they found. The largest tumor has shrunk "dramatically." His response was, "This is rare and very uncommon." In fact, he was so shocked by the shrinkage that he scheduled me for an immediate procedure to try to insert clips to mark the location of the tumors before they, as he put it, "completely disappear."

Stan's response to him was that there are "hundreds of people praying for her." Dr. T. pointed out that it has been proven that even when only a single person prays for another, it improves their prognosis. Stan replied, "Well, we have hundreds of people praying for Susan."

I will still have to take chemotherapy for the full six months. However, the long-term prognosis improves if the tumors shrink.

Dr. T. said, "Think shrink."

Stan replied, "Pray shrink."

Words cannot express my gratitude to those individuals praying for me. I hope one day I can pray for them as diligently as they have prayed for me.

Right now I am standing on top of the seesaw!

Dr. T. was also surprised I hadn't lost my hair. He noted to one of the interns how shocked he was that the tumor had shrunk that much and I still had hair. Maybe it will not fall out after all.

For the first time in my life, I knew I'd been the recipient of a miracle. I couldn't wait to get back to our room to call some of my prayer partners and church family and tell them the news.

We decided to celebrate by going out to eat. While at dinner, I began to feel weak and tired. My throat was getting sore. I opted for soup, Stan had steak.

Thanksgiving Hopes

The next day, Stan left again for Virginia to see the boys and to preach on Sunday. My brother came to stay with me.

Dr. T. had told us that if I continued to do well, he would let me go home for a visit during Thanksgiving. The thought of seeing the boys brought joy to my soul.

November 22

I have been hospitalized at MD Anderson. My blood count is very low (.04), and I continue to run a high fever. They are concerned I might have pneumonia. Overall, I feel completely miserable.

My doctor orders X-rays to be taken. As they wheel me into the staff elevator, a beautiful anesthesiologist walks in. She turns, looks at me with her infectious smile, and says, "You look so cute in your pink socks." Now I am feeling anything but *cute*. I know she was trying to encourage me, but I wanted to slap her. I am wearing a hospital gown that has had at least 2,000 washes. I've been on a morphine pump for three days. I can't remember when I've had a bath.

I just stare at her and she responds, "Be positive, God is going to take care of you." I nod and say thank you.

We continue down a few more floors. She then turns to me and says, "When you get back to your room, read Psalm 103."

I respond, "Bless the LORD, O my soul, and forget not all his benefits, who forgives all your sins and heals all your diseases."

Then she leans over and touches my arm. With her beautiful smile, she says, "God is going to heal you."

At that moment I felt strength come into my body— renewed strength.

Isn't it utterly amazing how God reveals Himself to us? We just have to be still. So many times in life I have been so focused on the mountain I am climbing that I miss the encounters with God along the way.

November 24

On Friday, November 19, I fell off the seesaw. I have spent the last four days in the hospital. I never realized how scary it is to be lying so sick in a hospital bed.

Saturday night I was so sick. I would just lie there and close my eyes and say the Twenty-third Psalm.

"Though I walk through the valley of the shadow of death…" I kept telling myself, "You just walk through the valley; you don't stay there." How comforting God's Word is at time of pain and suffering.

Today I am back on the seesaw, and soon I will be seeing life from the top again.

Joys of the journey—spending quality time with my brother, Brian. Why is it that it takes difficult trials in life to make us stop and spend quality time and express our love to those we care about the most?

After spending four days in the hospital, my hopes of going home to see the boys had washed away like the morning dew. Every day I would look at the family picture I tucked into my Bible. It was a picture a bystander had taken of us at the beach. I would close my eyes and feel the warm sand on my feet. I would listen for the sound of the ocean and the sounds of laughter and of love.

One day we'll be that happy again. I would tell myself this over and over again. I made a promise to myself that we would be at the beach again the following summer, happy and healthy.

I focused on the fact that, despite falling off the seesaw, I had remained strong. They were able to put clips around the tumor site, and I was able to take my treatment. I had stayed on track. I was determined not to miss a treatment.

Stan had once told a story in a sermon (a tale repeated from pastor and author Dr. Dale Galloway) of a shy, unassuming little guy named Chad. One winter's day Chad came home and told his mother he wanted to make Valentine cards for everyone in his class.

Her heart sank as he told her this, for she doubted any of his class-mates would give a card to Chad. She had watched these children coming home from school, talking and running and playing—but they never included Chad in their fun.

For the next few weeks, Chad and his mother worked tirelessly to craft thirty-five different cards to be given to his classmates. Valentine's Day finally arrived, and Chad excitedly loaded his handmade cards into his bag and bolted out the door.

Knowing this was going to be a tough day for Chad, his mother decided to have warm cookies and a glass of milk ready for him when he returned home. That afternoon, hearing children outside, she looked out the window. The children came laughing and play-ing as always. Chad was following behind—all alone again, though walking briskly.

She expected him to burst into tears as he came through the door with empty arms. As he stepped in, she quickly told him, "I have some warm cookies and milk for you."

But Chad seemed to hardly notice her words. As he walked by her, all he said was, "Not a one…not a single one!"

The mother's heart sank.

Then Chad added, with his face aglow, "*I didn't forget a one*, not a single one!" Little Chad had demonstrated the backward rules of the kingdom.

I was determined not to miss a treatment—not a single one.

While in the hospital, we'd been blessed with the visit of a volunteer chaplain. He was from a Baptist church in Houston. He was also a cancer survivor. His prayers were soothing and his visits were much appreciated. While I wasn't feeling like much for conversation, it was a great break in the day for my brother, who was there to stay with me.

After I was released from the hospital to return to the Rotary

House, this volunteer chaplain called to check on me and even invited me to have Thanksgiving dinner with his family. How hospitable to open your home to a cancer patient you don't even know for the holidays! Just what Jesus would do. I was so grateful for the invitation, but was too weak to have dinner away, and the doctor had given me strict orders to stay away from any germs and people.

A Different Holiday

Holidays in a hospital are different.

November 25

Thanksgiving Day. Stan and I spent the day here at the Rotary House. We had Thanksgiving lunch in the dining room downstairs. It was definitely different than any Thanksgiving I have ever had before. I am so grateful for the staff here who all work so hard to make our days brighter.

Traci brought us a "home cooked" Thanksgiving dinner for supper. It was so delicious! The first non-restaurant food I've had in a month!

We missed the boys but knew they were having a good time with our family in North Carolina.

Stan and I took a walk outside. The fresh air and sunshine were a wonderful contrast to the hospital room I had been staying in.

I cannot think about where I would like to be this Thanksgiving Day. Instead I have to work on getting my body stronger. So we can all be together next year for Thanksgiving.

Today, I was just thankful to be alive and spend the day with someone I loved and cared about and who loved me in return.

10

No More Bad Hair Days

I had come to realize I wasn't capable of taking care of the kids at this point in my life. I needed to take care of *me*, so that my sons would have a mother for the long term.

I began to focus on healing. I spent much time in prayer and reading my Bible. I also began to read anything I could get my hands on regarding breast cancer.

All the while I dedicated myself to lots of rest and no stress. I enjoyed the beauty of everything I saw, from the sunshine outside to the beautiful interiors of the hospital and of the Rotary House.

Rotary House had many activities to enjoy. I tried to take in as many as possible. We played Bingo on certain nights, did a craft one night, and watched a movie. Most of the time, we just socialized with other patients and their family members. As much as I missed home, I always felt "peace" here. The Rotary House was becoming my home away from home.

Stan and I discussed moving the kids to Houston to stay with us. Stan even looked into places where we could live close to the hospital and a kindergarten for Briggs. After much thought and prayer, we decided leaving them in Virginia would be the best alternative.

We would need someone else to stay with us to make that arrangement doable. Someone would need to stay with the kids while I took treatments and had doctor's appointments. Once again we decided that despite the difficulties of being separated, our family was strong, and we could do it.

Higher Places

To give the boys reassurance, Stan tried to fly home almost every weekend. I was blessed to have family and friends who would come and stay with me when he couldn't—as well as a renewed reminder of my prayer support from back home.

November 27

Today I received a package containing an interesting item—a beeper. I always did want one. This is not your ordinary beeper. It's a prayer beeper. A dear friend ordered this for me to have. What a cool gadget. Anytime someone prays for me they can call my beeper number and it will beep, letting me know someone, somewhere is lifting me up in prayer. Wow! I have never heard of such. Can't wait to get my first "beep!" A tangible reminder that I am loved by many people. Feeling blessed.

November 28

Today I am jealous of people who have a port-a-cath (a catheter that connects to a vein under the skin, usually in the chest). Craziness! The CVC line dangles down my chest and is so annoying and so much main- tenance. I just want to be able to take a shower and feel the water hit my face. It's the small things in life.

Every two days my CVC line has to be cleaned. I am proud I learned how to do this all by myself now, in case I am not in Houston for my nurse to care for or I'm not with Stan. The sterile procedure that I must perform is quite involved. Even though I have watched Nette, my nurse, do this many times, today I learned how to do it myself.

I go into the bathroom. Put a mask over my face and sterile gloves on my hands. The gloves come in an individual pack as to prevent any exposure to germs. I lay a sterile covering over the counter. Open the sterile box. Inside is a pair of scissors, tape, bandages for my chest, Hibiclens antimicrobial cleanser, cotton swabs to clean around the site, alcohol wipes, and gauze.

To do everything correctly and thoroughly, the process takes about 30 to 40 minutes. On top of that, I have to do a heparin flush to the CVC line every single day. (This medication will prevent blood clots from forming in the CVC line.) Until this journey started, I didn't even know what a port-a-cath or a CVC line even was.

Today, I find myself sitting in a hospital lounge, passing time away discussing with other patients how lucky they are to have a port while I have a CVC line. Life in the sick world.

On the bright side, I am accumulating quite a collection of scissors, because they can only be used once!

November 29

Today it happened. I woke up in a sea of hair. I knew what had to be done, but I just couldn't do it. Every time I turned the clippers on, the sound was horrendous, and my head was incredibly sore. At 9:00 p.m. I told myself I had to do it. I went into the bathroom alone and began to shave the back of my head. But to no avail.

As I lay in my bed unable to sleep, my prayer beeper went off about 1:00 a.m., and I knew someone was lifting me up in prayer at the exact time I needed it. Suddenly, words from Habakkuk came to my mind: "The LORD God is my strength; he makes my feet like the feet of a deer, and he enables me to go on to higher places" (Habakkuk 3:19).

At that moment I realized, "Susan, God is taking you to higher places—and you do not need hair to get there."

November 30

I got up early and went over to the hospital beauty shop by myself and had my head shaved. I asked the beautician to turn my chair around so I wouldn't have to watch. I couldn't stand for her to touch my head. It was so sore.

She applied some Sea Breeze astringent to my scalp and began shaving my head. I closed my eyes and told myself, *Be strong. You are in control of this. Don't let cancer control you.*

I could feel the hair falling off my head. The sound of the clippers caused me to grit my teeth. I just closed my eyes tighter.

She was finished. I placed a black cap over my head before turning my chair around to look into the mirror. I didn't really want to know what it looked like. It was a humbling experience.

Two hours later, I began another twenty-four-hour round of chemotherapy. After only 3 ccs (a teaspoon is 5 ccs) of chemo, I plummeted. I couldn't breathe, I had severe chest and abdominal pain, and eventually I broke out in hives.

Instantly doctors and nurses surrounded me in the chemo treatment room. They began giving me oxygen and pumping large doses of Benadryl through the CVC line.

Everything was blurring, and I kept hearing the nurse tell me to breathe. I opened my eyes and saw Stan standing outside the room looking in through the window. The concern in his eyes scared me.

I realized hair was the least of my worries.

"Do not be afraid of those who kill the body but cannot kill the soul. Rather, be afraid of the One who can destroy both the soul and the body in hell. Are not two sparrows sold for a penny? Yet not one of them will fall to the ground apart from the will of your Father. And even the very hairs of your head are all numbered. So don't be afraid; you are worth more than many sparrows" (Matthew 10:28–31).

After my adverse effects from Taxol, they sent me back to the Rotary House to rest. They scheduled me to try the chemo again the next day. I was exhausted and broken out in hives all over my body. How could such a tiny amount of a drug cause such a reaction? The thought of being hooked up again was frightening.

I went back and crashed, trying to entertain myself by detouring my brain to *Extreme Makeover*. Never being a TV watcher before, I really loved having some time to watch what I wanted. Even Stan was starting to get into it. *Extreme Makeover* along with old reruns of *Seinfeld* seemed to be our mainstay.

It was time to get ready for bed. I knew I had a hard day ahead of me tomorrow. I walked into the bathroom. I stared at myself in the mirror. I'd worn a little black cap to cover my baldness, with a wide-brim hat over that. I felt comfortable and confident in the new look. I continued to stare into the mirror. I was okay with how I looked with the little cap on. But what would I look like if I took it off?

The thought of baldness brought visions of true sickness. I didn't want to look like so many bald people I'd seen. I wasn't blessed with beautiful olive skin or striking eyes.

I decided I had faced enough today. With that, I left the little black cap on and got dressed for bed.

The next day, I watched as the line was attached. The nurse slowly turned on the chemo and I watched as it entered my body—then felt the rush of coldness. Fear was all around me. But everything went fine. Soon I drifted off to sleep and awoke when they told me it was time to go back to the hotel. I'd been there all day.

Much of what we fear never happens.

A Visit Home

The next day I finished another twenty-four-hour round of chemo. I was on different anti-nausea medicine and would return the next day to receive a Neulasta shot, which boosts white blood cells in the bone marrow, but also causes bone pain.

We had our doctor visit with Dr. T., and he seemed very pleased with how I was doing. Stan began discussing with him when he thought I could come home. I was kind of taken back because, while I missed the boys deeply, the thought of flying home was frightening and I wasn't sure my body was up to it. Dr. T. agreed to let me come home but explained that due to my blood-count pattern I needed to leave by tomorrow and stay close to an oncologist.

We left his office, and I just wanted to tar my feet to the Texas earth and not go anywhere. What was Stan thinking? I couldn't get on a plane.

Stan turned to me as we walked back to the room. "Susan, the boys need to see you." Well, maybe someone could fly them out here. "No, I think you need to go home. You can do it."

The rest of the afternoon we worked on making plans. We needed flights, and I particularly needed a front seat.

Medical access is limited in our small town. Our local hospital didn't have an oncologist, so the doctor thought it would be best for me to stay at my parents' home in North Carolina. I called a high school friend who was a radiologist, and she hooked us up with an oncologist in Asheville. We decided that after the flight to Asheville on Thursday, I would stay that night at my parents' house—a half-hour's drive from Asheville—then return the following day to meet with the new oncologist. He would oversee my treatments for the next two weeks before I returned to Houston.

As I got into the taxi to leave, I felt as if I were stepping into the river and hoping the waters would part. Donned in a hat, gloves, and a mask, I looked like someone with a rare communicable disease.

About an hour into the flight, my pain became intense. My neck, head, and teeth hurt terribly. I refused to take anything. My former experience with pain medicine had led me to believe I would rather be in pain than feel dizzy and confused.

After two hours and forty minutes, we landed in Asheville. I felt nauseated and had the taste of those anti-nausea pills in my mouth. What I would have given to be in my own bed. Better yet to be in Houston. I had so much confidence in my doctors there. I felt safe there. I had confidence they knew how to take care of me if I experienced problems. But what if something unexpected happened here in Asheville?

Finally, I was in bed that night at my parents' house. I awoke the next morning so sick I couldn't move. I heard a voice say, "Susan, you have to get up. We have to drive back to Asheville and see the doctor at 8:30." But I couldn't. Every inch of my body was sore from the Neulasta shot. I hadn't had anything for pain, and I was so nauseated I couldn't move. *O God, why did I come home?*

With Stan's constant pushing, I got up and tried to get my clothes on. I couldn't. I started to cry. "See if the doctor can see me later," I pleaded.

"Susan, they can't, and you have to take a treatment on Monday."

I climbed back into bed. I knew my body's limits.

Because I missed the doctor's appointment that day, it made me unable to have chemo administered there the following Monday. In fact, the doctor couldn't see me until the following Friday.

Why does everything have to be so difficult? I panicked. *What have I done?* I *had* to take my treatment that Monday.

Stan left for the four-hour drive to Virginia to get the boys. I couldn't believe I was in this situation.

Stan called our dear friend, Dr. Sutherland. He was able to

get the Herceptin I needed, and scheduled me for a treatment on Monday in Virginia. In the craziness of this journey, things seemed to work out.

About that moment, my bedroom door opened. It was my mom and dad, having driven from Virginia where they'd been staying at our house with the boys. Two things about this trip weighed heavy on my mind—seeing my parents and seeing my children. How would I look to them? I didn't want them to see me sick.

Mom came in and started to hug me. I was lying in my bed with my black cap on. It was a part of me now—kind of like the wedding band that you never take off.

The touch of her hug hurt, and I asked her not to touch me.

Daddy looked at me in those tender, hazel eyes. No parent wants to see his child sick.

Mom asked what I wanted to eat. I could think of nothing palatable at that moment. But she hurried downstairs into the kitchen to whip something up.

With both my parents in their seventies, I knew they were tired from their trip from Virginia.

"Let's see what your head looks like," Mom stated casually. "Is all your hair gone?" I was instantly defensive. No one had seen me bald except the beautician who kindly shaved me, and I planned to keep it that way.

"No, Mom, I'm not letting anyone see it."

"Oh."

My parents live in a two-story white old farmhouse. It belonged to my mother's parents. It's a place very dear to my heart. The thing I've always noticed about the home place is you can hear everything in it. My parents still use an old rotary dial phone in the hallway. I'm thirty-four years old, and it's been there all my life. Mom hadn't been home long before that phone started ringing. I'm sure she was trying to be discreet, but I could hear all her conversations. No doubt she was conversing with one of my aunts. Those women talk every day—about what, I'm not sure. My mom and her sisters are quite something; just think of *The Golden Girls*.

I overheard her telling Aunt Evelyn, "Yes, she's lost all her hair. She's wearing a little cap on her head, and she wouldn't let me see her head. I don't know why." She went on to talk about the boys and how Stan had gone to Virginia to pick them up, and would bring them there that night.

Stan had become like an actor in a traveling circus. From dad, to husband, to caregiver, to pastor, preacher, friend, son, son-in-law, launderer, cook, concierge, and counselor. I really don't know how he did it.

Seeing the Boys

At 6:30 that evening, Stan called to inform me he was in Asheville. In other words, *Get up and get yourself ready; your kids will be there in thirty minutes.* My body hurt, and I'd always believed the best cure for nausea was to not move. I took a pain pill and some more anti-nausea meds. Then I forced myself to get up. I carefully looked at what I might wear. I'd been carrying the same clothes since I left Virginia six weeks earlier, when I packed for only a week.

I headed to the bathroom to apply some makeup. Next the wig. I'd spent $300 on a wig and never worn it. It just didn't seem right. Besides, my head stayed so sore I didn't want to wear the scratchy thing.

I fit it on and stared at myself in the mirror. Did I look sick? Did I look different? *Who are you kidding? You look a lot different.* I don't care how much money you spend on a wig, it never looks exactly like you and your hair.

I heard Stan pull into the driveway, and I slowly made my way down the stairs. I sat in the chair in my parents' entryway. Slowly the door opened, and in walked Briggs and Glenn.

I smiled big and said, "Hey guys!" just as if we were all back home after a normal day of work and school and play.

For a moment, the boys both just stared at me. There was no expression on their faces. Inside I wanted to cry streams of tears, but I stayed with the plan to appear cheery.

After what seemed like minutes—though it was probably only seconds—Glenn ran to me and flung his little arms around me, not saying a word.

"Your mother is sore," my dad warned; "don't touch her so rough and hard." But I nodded my father away, and Glenn kept his little face buried into my neck. He never moved for several minutes.

Slowly, Briggs came over and hugged my other side. I quickly tried to engage in conversation with him. "How was school today?... I'm so glad to see you.... I've missed you so much.... Look how you've grown!"

I could tell that Briggs, in his reflective manner, was trying to process all that was happening, and he was weighing every adult's response.

My mother summoned us to the kitchen for the dinner she'd been preparing all afternoon. After I stomached a light meal and put on a front to the boys, saying I was fine, I finally excused myself to "take some medicine." I could hardly wait to lie down. I slowly walked upstairs, went into my bedroom, and shut the door.

I shed the wig and put on my soft cap. The wig must have worked, for the boys never mentioned my hair, but Briggs did eye me again and again.

I popped some more pain medicine and anti-nausea drugs, and lay down. No sooner had I closed my eyes than I opened them to see two little boys sneaking into my room. They stared, and I panicked. Laying beside my bed was my wig!

I noticed as their eyes widened. Glenn, in his innocence of age three, pointed to the wig and exclaimed, "Mommy, the medicine made all your hair fall out!" Before I could think through my response, Briggs added, "Daddy told us you were going to take medicine that would make your hair fall out."

"Yes," I told them, "the doctors are giving me medicine to make my boo-boos better, and the medicine makes your hair fall out." Their eyes moved from a reaction of shock to "That's neat."

I told them again how much I loved them and missed them. They hugged me on the bed.

Briggs glanced over at the wig, trying to put it all together. About that time, Stan realized they'd escaped and called them back to the dinner table for dessert. Quickly, they scurried downstairs.

December 3

Joys of the journey—seeing Briggs and Glenn.

Anticipating seeing Briggs and Glenn was a cross between Christmas Eve as a child and a first date. I was so excited about seeing the boys but nervous too. I knew I looked sick, and I did everything I could to look my best. I wanted their approval that Mommy looked okay.

End result: *Priceless* (a definite MasterCard moment!)

I will never forget the love I received from my boys after being away for so long. God continues to show me that love is a powerful form of healing.

11

How the Grinch Stole Christmas

The next Sunday, we packed up and headed home to Virginia. My soreness from the Neulasta shot made the four-hour trip seem much longer. I also had a knot in my stomach about returning home.

First, I felt emotional.

Second, I knew my home had experienced a "makeover," and I was nervous about what that would be. One of the small groups in our church had redecorated it as part of our "forty days of community."

Third, there was the house itself. For years I'd been concerned about our home. There was the mold and the suspicious drinking water, plus the gassy stuff coming out of the hill behind our house. Living in a rural, coal-mining area, I had tried to find an environmental group that would assess our home when Briggs was born five years earlier. I couldn't find anyone who wouldn't charge an absurd amount of money. I recalled in my mind telling Stan the night I was diagnosed that I wanted out of that house. Maybe I was grasping for straws, wanting to find something to blame for the disease.

On this day, however, when I entered my home, I felt love.

Better Together

As soon as we drove up the driveway, the boys were ecstatic to see our Christmas yard art—an inflated Grinch. It wasn't my usual decorating style, but seeing how much the boys loved it, I began to rethink some of my ways.

As we entered the home, Briggs was beaming as he told me of the "redo."

Everything was lit up with little white lights, complete with a tree in our den. This was more Christmas decorations than I'd had in ten years combined. The boys thought it was paradise.

We strolled through the hallway and admired the newly painted walls and rearrangement of furniture.

Then I walked into my bedroom. What a transformation! Our cream walls were now celery with a beautiful cream spread and lots of pillows and airy white shears over the windows. Above our chest of drawers were framed baby pictures of Stan and me. I'd had them laying aside ever since Briggs's baby shower with the intention of framing them.

I felt a tear in the corner of my eye.

As my eyes moved across the room, I noticed a plaque on the mill chest with the word *Believe*. Once again my eyes filled with tears.

The room was cozy, warm, and stylish—more than I ever imagined. It was done out of love, and through that love, it seemed to radiate positive energy and healing.

I thought, *We truly are better together. Always.*

I affirmed to the boys the wonder of it all, and went to sit in the recliner and watch them tell me about the Christmas decorations that put twinkles in their eyes. I fell asleep in my new bedroom surrounded by love.

On Monday morning, Stan took me to Buchanan General

Hospital for my first treatment away from MD Anderson. I felt a little nervous about being in a new place for treatment, although I knew Dr. Sutherland would take exceptional care of me. I was also nervous about seeing friends and acquaintances for the first time since my treatment started.

I put on my cute little black hat and applied some makeup and lipstick.

As we walked in the door at the hospital, the first person I saw was our friend Eugene. He approached us and hugged Stan, and his brown eyes showed his empathy and concern. *Great friends are blessings in life we often overlook.*

Dr. Sutherland came in, hugged me, and then assessed my blood. All looked good, and we began the treatment.

One more down.

I spent two days at home, then Stan took me back to North Carolina before my blood count would plummet and I got sick. Poor Stan just lived in his vehicle. I'm so thankful God had blessed us with a new one several months before I got sick.

In North Carolina, I finally got another appointment with the oncologist in Asheville who would oversee my care while I was away from Houston. Dr. C. was a kind, younger doctor very interested in the clinical trial I was doing.

Stan drove back to Virginia to preach on Sunday and be with the boys. Sunday night he came back to North Carolina to take me to yet another chemo treatment. I don't know who wrote the traditional wedding vows, but I'm not sure any of us understand them when we say, "in sickness and in health."

My first chemo at the Asheville Cancer Center went well. That weekend I was scheduled to fly with my mother and brother back to Houston for another twenty-four-hour round of the chemo Taxol the following Monday.

As I enjoyed the neighborhood Christmas lights in North Carolina, I prayed that God would grant me the blessing of being with my boys for Christmas. It was December 18, and I hadn't bought the first gift. The giving and receiving of gifts seemed far from my mind, but the essence of just being with people I love was a deeper joy than ever.

What about Christmas?

Back in Texas.

December 19

> I went down to the front desk today and received a large envelope of mail. How exciting! The front desk personnel at the Rotary House always knows my name. Today, I tell them how impressed I am that they can always recall my name. Instantly, the lady assisting me responds, "You always receive the *most* mail!"
>
> Wow! My whole body smiles. There are more than 300 rooms at the Rotary House, and I receive the most mail! I feel loved beyond measure. This has to be as good for my body as a chemo treatment.
>
> Tonight in my room, I look over all my cards again. So many people. So faithful to send me well wishes. One Sunday school class sends me a card every week. I never knew such a simple act of kindness could mean so much to someone.
>
> I have a box with all my cards. I save every one.

December 20

As I write, I am listening to a piano student play "O Holy Night" here at MD Anderson Cancer Center. It is absolutely beautiful. The music has put me in the most wonderful spirit of Christmas.

Many Sundays I have heard Stan say from the pulpit, "It is not by accident that you are here at church today." That is the way I feel about being at MD Anderson this Christmas. In a very God-like way, I feel this is exactly where I am supposed to be today. Obviously, it is not a place I would plan or intend to be.

Joys of the journey—I've found that sick people can have a lot of fun together, especially when I am one of them! One of the reasons God has placed me here is to show my new friends that Christmas is not about being at a certain place, with certain people, eating a certain meal. During the last two months, I have made a lot of friends here at the Rotary House. Many are from other countries, such as Jordan, Spain, and Brazil. Obviously, everyone wants to spend Christmas at home with family and close friends. To some of my new friends, this makes them bitter and unhappy at Christmastime.

While being with friends and family is my favorite part of Christmas, experiencing Christmas is about something much different.

Christmas is about the tender mercies of God. God loved us enough to send His only begotten Son to be Savior of the world, and He is with us no matter where we are or who we are with this Christmas.

Read the Christmas story. It's not all happy. This year I

have focused on the character of Joseph. The Bible says very little about Joseph. Imagine how humiliating and heartbreaking his discovery of Mary's pregnancy must have been. He would have a child at a time of national anguish. Then, to top it off, he had to have his firstborn child in a lowly stable. But God turned Joseph's heartbreaking experience into something wonderful.

Like Joseph, everyone faces heartaches not of their own making. It has been said that "Every Bethlehem concludes with wise men kneeling and angels singing."

This Christmas I am experiencing Bethlehem!

That night was the boys' Christmas play. They were both cows. I hoped they did well, and I looked forward to seeing pictures of my little actors. I'd come to accept that I couldn't be a part of their many activities. However, one day I would be well, and all those things would have renewed meaning and joy.

Monday morning I arose and prayed that God would be with me that day, that I would not have any adverse reaction to the Taxol, and that my body would tolerate the chemo well so I would be able to go home for Christmas. Above all, I prayed that God's will would be done in my life.

My brother escorted me to take my chemo. He felt a little apprehensive, as I could only imagine how Stan had drilled him on what to make sure they did.

Twenty-four hours later, the chemo was completed—uneventfully. I would meet with the doctors the next day to see if I could come home.

I was discharged from the hospital on December 23 at 4:22 p.m. I had to leave the Rotary House by 4:30 in order to catch my flight. I felt the prayers of my many friends and family as my prayer beeper kept going off.

We made it home without a hitch—luggage and all.

December 25

Merry Christmas! How much fun seeing the boys' faces as they anticipated the toys Santa has left. A motorcycle bike for Glenn, a Game Boy for Briggs, and much more. Going to Stan's parents' home was fun, and it was so good to see everyone. How kind and giving our families have been to us. I can't forget Granddaddy's beautiful tree. An icon in the Briggs family Christmas for as long as I can remember!

Happy birthday, Jesus!

This Christmas I didn't buy a gift or go to a party or stress over the busyness of the season. Instead, I just experienced Christmas in my heart and soul and offered gifts of myself to God. I hope I never go back to the stress-filled, consumer Christmas.

12

The Seesaw

I was discovering that getting well wasn't just a physical process. It meant also facing the ups and downs of my emotions. I couldn't be physically well until I was also emotionally well.

December 27

Today, I had my eighth treatment in North Carolina. Stan went with me.

It was the usual protocol. I sit in the waiting room until my name is called. Then I proceed to have the nurse record my weight and blood pressure and draw my blood. Then I am ushered into a room to lie down and wait.

The nurse brings in the bags of premeds and chemo. As is procedure with us, Stan will examine each bag and read aloud each drug to make sure it matches what is listed on my treatment orders. Much to our surprise, the bag contains double the amount of my usual dosage. We question the nurse. She is sure it is correct. We are sure it is *not*.

The nurse returns with a new bag from the pharmacy. We were right; the dosage was vastly incorrect.

I will never forget what she told us. "This is the first mistake like this we have made all year." While I hope that is true, I wondered if this was just the first mistake anyone caught this year.

I don't mean to criticize anyone in the medical profession. I'm beyond grateful for the care, expertise, and kindness with which I was treated by so many in the medical field. I continue to have a deep appreciation for what they do, the hours they work, and the stress involved. However, none of us is beyond making errors, even when we have procedures in place designed to prevent them.

That being said, I also want to educate and encourage all patients to be advocates for their own health. A cancer survivor who practices law in Houston advised me to get my treatment orders from my oncologist and check every drug they put into my IV, to make sure the right drug and amount were always given. It was great advice.

Love Heals

My journal from those winter months reflected the continued ups and downs of my seesaw existence.

December 30

I called the doctor's office in Houston today. I have a cold I can't fight off. As I was going through my black notebook to find the number I came across the ultrasound report from May. As I compared it to the ultrasound report from October, I became so upset about what was and is and how different things could have been.

I lay on my bed reliving the things I could have done differently. I called Stan and cried.

I looked over and picked up a book my nurse, Nette, in Houston had given me. It was written by a surgeon at Yale. Scattered among all the research and medical terminology was this statement: "Unconditional love is the most powerful stimulant of the immune system. The truth is: love heals."

I began to relive the "utterly amazing" ways God has worked in my life since October 20. I recounted all the sacrifices, prayers, and unconditional love that has surrounded my family during this journey.

I got up and decided to open a package a friend had sent me. Inside was a pin that said, "Ewe are loved." Amazed and humbled, I realized God was again showing me the powerful healing of love.

My New Year's resolution: Recognizing that healing comes in many forms, not all physical. I commit to find at least three people in need and love them unconditionally.

January 9

"At least there is hope for a tree; if it is cut down, it will sprout again, and its new shoots will not fail. Its roots may grow old in the ground and its stump die in the soil, yet at the scent of water it will bud and put forth shoots like a plant" (Job 14:7–9).

I read this verse today and cannot get it out of my mind. I thought of how much I love trees. I thought of the tree that Brian and I used to climb and play in as kids. The hemlock tree that held our swing. The stumps in the "rock pasture" that we hid behind when we played cowboys and Indians. The tree that stopped the truck I was driving from turning over again. My favorite tree on North Campus of the University of Georgia where Stan proposed to me and carved our initials.

On October 20, 2004—the day I was diagnosed with cancer—the beautiful autumn foliage surrounded me all through Buchanan County.

I felt as if God was telling me that at the scent of water I would bud again. And as spring brings forth new shoots, so will my body—shoots that will not fail.

January 11

I spent time in the library today at MD Anderson reading any medical journal I could find on breast cancer. New research is just in on the dose-density trial at Johns Hopkins, a treatment option that I considered. It is early in the trial, but doctors feel that the initial results are very promising. A dose-density trial gives the patient chemo treatments every two weeks instead of every three weeks. They take the same amount of chemo in a shorter time period.

As I read this article, my heart gets tight and I have a

moment of panic. My mind shouts, "You should have done this trial!" I instantly get on the Internet to see what I can find. It's a war of the voices in my mind. I tell myself to relax and believe in the path I have taken and trust that the Lord is guiding me. But the other voice in my mind keeps repeating, "You made a mistake. Maybe God wasn't leading you here."

I think of my "No Regrets!" T-shirt. I relive conversations Stan and I have had on many occasions, promising each other to live this life with "no regrets."

As I sit here, thoughts of fear and regret fill my mind. Have I made the wrong decision?

In my room tonight I focused my mind on promises of God found in the Bible.

"I will never leave you nor forsake you" (Hebrews 13:5).

"Draw near to God and He will draw near to you" (James 4:8).

"Fear not, for I am with you; be not dismayed, for I am your God. I will strengthen you, yes, I will help you, I will uphold you with my righteous right hand" (Isaiah 41:10).

"You cannot add any time to your life by worrying about it" (Matthew 6:27).

"Come to me, all you who are weary and burdened, and I will give you rest" (Matthew 11:28).

I ended with reading Habakkuk 1:5. I don't completely understand what God is trying to show me through this verse and book, however I know without a shadow of doubt that the God of the universe sent it to *me* on October 23.

January 12

What a blessed week we have had in Houston. I met with the oncologist, who through physical exam felt the tumors were continuing to shrink. My treatment has gone exceptionally well, and we are scheduled to fly back to North Carolina tonight, leaving at 7:15 p.m.

This morning we met with the genetics specialist. Several weeks ago, I went through genetic testing. I was shocked that the insurance companies would not cover this, especially because the testing is $3,000.

Today was the day to get my results. I must admit I had a few knots in my stomach. I remembered when I took my securities license in Texas years ago, you had to press the enter button at the end to see immediately if you passed. I felt the same uncertain feeling. Do I want to know or not?

This time I had to open an envelope. In large bold letters were printed *Negative!* Not only had I appreciated the beeps this morning, but I was grateful for the diligent and faithful prayers.

Utterly amazing!

January 18

Here I am staying at my in-laws. I am sick. The events of the last week have left me in situations I never imagined.

We arrive in Virginia on Friday, and my heart is shattered to find the boys sick. I so desperately wanted to see their sparkling eyes and play with them.

Stan takes me to Glen and Pauline Smith's home, where I stay for three nights, then they drive me to Johnson City, Tennessee, where Brian meets us and takes me on to North Carolina. Mom and Dad are both sick, so I am staying at my in-laws.

Being in anyone's home when you are sick is not desirable. You long for your own room, your own bed.

January 19

Tonight I say a prayer of thanksgiving for Tami Viers. I don't know how we would have managed the last three months without her help keeping the boys. Her loving care of my children *even* when they are sick has been an indescribable comfort to me as their mom.

January 20

I'm sitting here at Glen and Pauline's again. I have made my rounds staying with people this week. It's snowing outside, and I've been relaxing on the couch—knitting. Suddenly, I feel like an old woman. I'm actually proud of myself for learning to knit and look forward to when I finish my first scarf! Everyone needs a hobby, and I'm certainly not void of that category.

During my stay with Stan's parents, Grandpa taught me how to relax. I don't mean just sitting down with nothing to do, but viewing life and its activities in a relaxing way.

I pray for Briggs and Glenn. That God would protect them and that Stan and I would plant God's Word into their lives. May they each ask Christ into their lives at an early age. May I be the mother who they each need, loving and accepting them for whom they are. May God's richest blessings surround them all the days of their lives.

January 22

I awoke and my eyes were met by two sparkling brown eyes. His hand rubbed the cap that covered my head. Then, the small soft, cold hand of my three year old rubbed my face twice. As Glenn looked at me, he said in his sweet voice, "You can't get sick in heaven. Daddy said so."

Briggs and Glenn, you are sun in my rain.

Shrinking Tumors

More journal entries continued to record my hopeful journey toward a new springtime.

January 31

I go to have my mammogram. During the first set of films, the doctor was not satisfied with the pictures so I had to have the entire process redone.

Two hours later, I am finished. As the technician announces I can go back to the dressing room, she stops and asks me a question, "Are you a Christian?"

I respond, "Yes."

She says, "I thought so [pause] by your smile." She then came over and put her arm around my shoulder and quoted Isaiah 43, "When you walk through the fire, you will not burn, when you pass through the waters, they will not sweep over you." She then squeezed my shoulder and whispered, "God bless you," and left the room.

I sat there for a moment, shocked. "Am I in some kind of dream?"

I'm wearing a hospital gown with silver hoop earrings. Nothing about me says Christian. After all the time I had spent with the technician, we had not engaged in any conversation other than the usual pleasantries. She was very focused on getting good films, and I wanted to encourage that concentrated effort.

Sometimes I feel as if I'm walking through a world I've never known and God keeps appearing to me. On this day when I am anxious about the tests being done and anticipating a new regimen of chemo, there He is closer than ever before.

February 1

Consultation for test results. I already knew in my heart but was overcome with awe when I read it on paper as the doctor visited with us: "There has been a significant response to the chemotherapy. There is marked change in the size of the tumors." At this point, the tumors are barely recognizable!

After three months of diligently praying "Shrink," God has answered our prayers in the manner in which we asked. I celebrate answered prayers and the completion of one-half of my chemo treatment.

Today, I have entered a new phase. I have started another three-month course of chemotherapy and begin a new prayer: "Lord, at the time of surgery I pray that not *one bad cell* will be found in my body."

He continues to be the author and perfecter of our faith.

Shouting from the top of the seesaw, "Utterly amazed!"

February 3

I'm sick. I can't even lift my head off the pillow. Nauseated to a level I've never experienced. I have been in bed for forty-eight hours. I haven't had a bath in two days. I was so sick last night that Mom slept with me. Oh, God, where are you? I don't want to be sick anymore.

February 10

I remember as kids back at Lake Junaluska playground playing on the seesaw. Last week I had one of those playground experiences where your seesaw partner was twenty pounds lighter than you! Remember how quickly you come down. Ouch! It always did hurt when you hit the ground.

I'm still on the old two-by-four wooden seesaw (not the plastic Little Tikes version my children enjoy). I remember it was always a struggle to get back to the top. No matter how hard I pushed with my feet, it was always a quick descent back to the ground.

Then, I began to see life from the top again and realized that just like the footprints in the sand, He was lifting me to the top!

February 12

Glenn's birthday! How much fun we had. All of the cousins were present. Making sand art and topping it with our treasure—a shark's tooth. My Aunt Gerry would be so pleased. She helped me find them on the beach in Florida twenty-five years ago. To think I've had those shark's teeth in a jar in my room for that many years. It seems so long ago. I pray God would grant me good health for another twenty-five years and beyond!

Glenn liked his "Glenn" Bay Packer cake and blew out his candles with such determination. To announce his maturity of another year, he asked a profound question at dinner tonight, "Mama, who made God?"

Happy fourth birthday, Glenn.

I love you.

February 14

I'm sitting here at the Western North Carolina Cancer Center ready for my fifteenth treatment. As I look around the room full of chairs with people hooked up to chemo pumps, it occurs to me that I am the only person here under the age of sixty.

Welcome to the world of gerontology! Due to the fact that my blood counts stay low, they put me in a private room. As much as I love being with people, I prefer to take my treatments in private.

Today is Valentine's Day. The "love" holiday. How blessed I feel today to be loved. "And the greatest of these is love" (1 Corinthians 13:13). As many times as I have read that verse and believed it, today I understand it.

February 15

Glenn and I are playing today while Briggs is at school. We were singing "Fuzzy Wuzzy was a bear. Fuzzy Wuzzy had no hair." Glenn stopped and looked at me and says, "Mama, you're Fuzzy Wuzzy!"

February 17

Back in Houston. I went by the chemotherapy unit to see if I could get my schedule changed. The nurse told me it was "impossible." They were overbooked for Monday, and I would have to keep the time I had.

I need to change the time so that I can leave within twenty-four hours of finishing my chemo treatment.

If I don't fly out by that time, then I'm too sick to fly for days.

Tonight I read in my Bible about how "all things are possible with God." Then I read about Joseph and how "the favor of God was upon him" (Genesis 39:21).

Lord, I pray that I will never forget that *all* things are possible with You. May Your favor rest upon my shoulders. Amen.

February 18

This afternoon I went by the chemotherapy unit again to try my "luck." The waiting room was packed with the same two attendants working. As the line dissipated, I made my way to the front to speak with the attendant whom I did not speak with yesterday. I told her my story and asked if there was any way I might be able to change my schedule.

She responded, "We're booked."

I replied. "I know."

She then asked, "Do you believe anything is possible?"

I looked her in the eyes and said, "All things are possible with God." She smiled, and I continued, "and I believe His favor is resting on my shoulder."

The other attendant turned and gave her a look. She continued looking on the computer. Then, she lifted her head and mouthed to me, "9:30 a.m."

I smiled and mouthed back to her, "Perfect."

She then stood up and placed her hand over mine

giving it a squeeze. Instantly, I thought of the power of touch. Leaning inward, she gently smiled and said, "God bless you. Always believe in prayer, and worry not."

I responded, "I will, and God bless you. I'll see you Monday."

I left the unit thinking, "Did I just say that to a total stranger?" Then I felt as if God's favor was resting on my shoulder, and I could reach out and touch *Him*.

Another Life, Another Story

I met some incredible people. Every day now, I think of Morgan.

February 18—evening entry

Today I met a girl named Morgan. I had seen her at the Rotary House a few weeks ago. We were riding the elevator together, and I decided to introduce myself. She is a beautiful twenty-three-year-old from Fort Walton, Florida. She has inflammatory breast cancer and was first misdiagnosed.

As she told me her story, I was so saddened and at the same time so grateful for my past years of health. She is a newlywed and has gone through four months of chemo and then a mastectomy without reconstruction, because she is not a candidate at this time.

She shared with me how after her PET scan, the doctor described the results as "my whole body lit up like a Christmas tree."

I wanted to hug her and cry—and tell her it will be all right.

Stan and I played Bingo tonight with Morgan and her husband, Mark. We enjoyed visiting with them, and I prayed God would heal her body completely.

From a year later:

Morgan Reneé (Perkins) Welch
May 18, 1981—January 29, 2006

Morgan Reneé (Perkins) Welch, age 24, of Fort Walton Beach, Florida, passed away peacefully January 29, 2006, surrounded by family.

Morgan was born May 18, 1981, and had recently moved with her husband, Mark, to San Antonio, Texas.

Morgan graduated with honors from Fort Walton Beach High School in 1999. She went on to graduate cum laude with a B.S. in Music Therapy from William Carey College in Hattiesburg, Mississippi. Morgan was selected to intern at the Maryland School for the Blind in Baltimore, Maryland. While working for the Okaloosa County Schools in the Blended School, Morgan touched souls with her gift of music and was passionate about her work with children, especially in the field of Music Therapy with developmentally disabled children.

Morgan is survived by her loving husband, SSgt Mark Welch; father, Craig Perkins and wife, Tracy; mother, Pamela Morgan and Chuck Touchton; step-sister, Jamie Walker; step-brother, Robbie Walker;

grandparents, Lt. Col. Larry Perkins (Ret.) and wife, Yvonne; grandmother, Laverne Prevratil; uncles and aunts, Roy and Cindy Frazier, Mike and Debbie Riley, and Scott and Theresa Perkins; and cousins, Ryan Gore and wife, Kelly, Lisa Carr and husband, Adam, Heath Riley, and Katie Rose Perkins.

A Celebration of Life will be held Thursday, February 2, 2006, at 10 a.m. at the First Baptist Church of Mary Esther with Pastor Joe Plott officiating. Interment will follow at Heritage Gardens Cemetery in Niceville, Florida.

In lieu of flowers, the family has requested that contributions be made to the Morgan Welch Music Therapy Scholarship Fund, c/o Heritage Bible Church, 2323 Mt. Vernon Ave., Bakersfield, CA 93306.

We would like to offer our deepest gratitude and appreciation to the United States Air Force for their compassion and understanding during a very trying time.

We would also like to thank our many friends and family and Heritage Bible Church family for their generous support throughout this journey.... "I have fought the good fight, I have finished the race, I have kept the faith" (2 Timothy 4:7).

—*The Bakersfield Californian*, February 2, 2006

Morgan's legacy—the Morgan Welch Inflammatory Breast Cancer Research Program and Clinic, a new service of MD Anderson—was opened later in 2006. [For more information, access "Inflammatory

Breast Cancer Research Program" at the MD Anderson Center website—www.mdanderson.org.]

> Weeks before her wedding, Morgan Welch noticed that one of her breasts appeared to have a mosquito bite. She had absolutely no idea that it was a sign of a rare, aggressive form of breast cancer – a disease that often spreads before women realize it. After antibiotics did nothing to alleviate symptoms that she thought were caused by a breast infection, Welch was diagnosed with inflammatory breast cancer (IBC). . . .

> Welch received chemotherapy and improved enough to undergo surgery to remove the tumor. Doctors hoped she would improve with a combination of chemotherapy, radiation and hormonal treatment. It worked for a while and then the cancer progressed. . . .

> "When Morgan was in the hospital the last time, I took Dr. Cristofanilli out in the hall and said, 'For what it's worth, don't let this hinder you. This is a bigger fight than just for Morgan, just for us,'" says Mark Welch, Morgan's widower. "I made him promise that he would continue to learn more about this disease and do everything he could to offer women with IBC more hope."

> Welch continuously motivates Cristofanilli in his quest for better outcomes for women with IBC: he carries Morgan's wedding photo in his shirt pocket every day.

> —MDAnderson Cancer Center, "Newsroom," October 25, 2007

Several years later, someone we knew would travel to Houston to become a patient at the Morgan Welch Inflammatory Breast Cancer Center. She lived and would receive the outcome and hope Morgan had dreamed of. Utterly amazing.

13

Unconditional Love

Brian's news was painful, because I knew I couldn't fix it. In fact, I couldn't fix my own pain.

February 19

Brian tells me over the phone today that his marriage is ending. I try to encourage him and demonstrate my love. I hang up with him and just cry. I feel engulfed with anxiety and stress that causes me physical pain. Oh, God, how can all of this be happening?

February 20

I still can't get the divorce out of my mind. How do I help?

Today I realize my helplessness. I can't fix Brian's marriage. I can't fix my body. I don't know why I ever thought I could control the things around me.

Today I feel like I don't know who I am anymore. When did I stop making decisions? I've become so accustomed to trying to please everyone or trying to impress others that I don't even know what Susan wants.

Lord, how do I move forward to change these things? Help me. Show me. Give me strength. Give me courage. I want to be different. I want to be the person You created me to be.

All in a Phone Booth

How gracious of God to brighten our journey through dark trials with incidents that later bring laughter-laden memories.

February 21

Laughter for the Journey—Stan and I usher into Bush International Airport with bags in hand. It's 6:00 p.m., and our plane is scheduled to leave at 7:15 p.m. We have fifteen minutes to find a location. We are a couple with a mission. At 6:15 p.m., Stan will have to give me a shot of Neulasta. Where in the world can we look inconspicuous? I will have to remove my coat and pull up my sleeve. Stan will have to put on surgical gloves, take out the alcohol wipes and the ever-important syringe.

What would you think if you were a bystander? Let alone a security guard!

Stan finds, in his opinion, the perfect place—a telephone booth! Can you imagine six-foot, four-inch Stan and me crammed into a telephone booth? It was about as hilarious as Stan and me in a bathtub with a mattress over our heads during a tornado when we lived in Fort Worth, Texas.

We make our way inside the telephone booth. We're ready. Sleeve up. Alcohol wipes out. Gloves on and syringe in hand. I laugh a nervous laugh. I can't believe I'm letting Stan give me a shot—and, of all places, in a telephone booth. We are ready for the moment of truth—but Stan can't get the top off the needle. In normal circumstances I would say just work with it until you force it off. Not today. I'm in an airport. Where could I get another shot if he messes this one up? Not to mention this one shot costs $3,200. (I know. I also thought the pharmacy had too many zeros in it.)

I politely ask, "Where are the instructions?" Stan responds," In my back pocket." I just look at my spouse with one of those long, blank stares.

So, out of the telephone booth Stan goes, pulls out the instructions, and wedges back in. This time he successfully removes the cover.

In seconds, which seemed like minutes, it was over.

We stumble out of the booth. I straighten my clothes and try to give the ever-calm "nothing has happened" appearance, all the while wondering what the guy on the cell phone must be telling the caller on the other end. Picture it. The whole event could be an episode of *Seinfeld*.

February 21, evening

Flight CO2386 Houston to Asheville. It's a small Express plane and a turbulent ride. I'm nauseated and having hot flashes. I'm praying we will land soon.

As we prepare for the final descent, turbulence worsens. I realize I'm not going to make it. I bend over to get the plastic bag I always carry only to discover I left it in the carry-on bag. Panicked, I look for the nausea bag. *None.* I gaze at Stan and whisper, "I'm sick." No time left. I turn to the aisle and began vomiting into my hands. A kind, red-headed lady across the aisle quickly hands me her nausea bag. I continue. She then places her hand on my shoulder and begins to rub my back with the touch that only a mother has. She whispers to me, "You're so courageous." She then hands me tissues and napkins out of her purse. The plane lands.

God is always with us. Tonight His presence was channeled through a lady's hands and words.

Utterly amazing.

March 6

After a three-hour drive from Vansant while running a fever of 102 degrees, I was admitted to St. Joseph's Hospital in Asheville, North Carolina, for neutropenic fever and infection. Today I was discharged.

Our Daily Bread devotion for March 4 reads:

"'He gives power to the weak, and to those who have no might He increases strength' (Isaiah 40:29). Researchers at the University of Virginia have found that most people perceive a hill to be steeper than it really is, especially if they're tired or carrying a heavy load. When asked to estimate the slope of a hill, test participants consistently misjudged it, thinking a ten-degree slant was about thirty degrees, and rating a five-degree slope as nearly twenty degrees."

As I lay in the hospital Friday night, I was one of those participants. My mountain seemed to be getting steeper, and my body had endured enough.

I told Stan I could not tolerate seven more weeks of chemotherapy. They would have to lower my dosage.

Tonight I have refocused. Realizing that victims sit down and focus on the mountain, I intend to be a *survivor.*

March 7

Today I took my eighteenth treatment. As I lay in the chair with chemo flowing through my veins, I began to reflect. I thought of our church's building fund, Stan's challenge for a financial sacrifice. A month before my diagnosis, Stan and I had given $5,000 to the fund. I thought of all the monetary gifts given to help me offset the enormous expense of my illness. Three different people, at three different times, gave us that same amount—$5,000.

God had repaid my sacrifices threefold and then some. God had not only placed people in my life, but those individuals had been open to God's direction of sacrifice so that I might live.

March 8

Joys of the journey—standing in the bathroom looking in the mirror, I'm startled to see an acquaintance of mine—Blackie.

It all began about seven years ago when I looked in the mirror one morning and gasped to find a hair growing from my chin! Since that day, we have been at war with a pair of Twissors as my weapon of defense. Blackie— the cell that seventeen weeks of chemotherapy can't even kill. I panic. If this cell is still alive, what other "bad cells" in my body is the chemo not killing?

I regain calmness and again focus into the mirror. Blackie is a survivor.

The Struggle for Strength

Spring drew near, full of promise—adding to my longing for a restored and revitalized body.

March 10

Today I am feeling stronger, though I am too weak to travel back to Texas for my next treatment. I am pleased to be able to take my next FEC combination chemo treatment in Asheville on Monday. It will allow me more time to rest.

One afternoon while I was in the hospital, I began to think about my upcoming surgery options. For some reason I think I need to have my MRI that was performed in October reviewed. I discuss it with Stan and decide I will contact Duke and have the report sent to Houston.

March 11

On Monday when I took my treatment, I ran into a childhood friend's parents as we were leaving the hospital in Asheville. I will never forget the look on their faces when they saw me. How shocked they were that I was sick, and, after spending the weekend in the hospital, I could have been a poster child for cancer.

I ached inside at the reality of my disease. I hurt for them hurting for me. I just want to look normal so I can mask what's going on inside my body.

March 12

It's snowing outside. I can see the purple crocuses blooming as the snow falls. I realize that spring is coming but there is still some winter to endure. So it is with my body.

I continue to focus on the crocus. The purple flower has been welcoming spring to my mother's yard for forty years. My grandmother planted them. She died more than twenty years ago. Isn't it interesting how the seeds we sow outlive us?

May I be ever mindful of the seeds my life is sowing.

March 19

I'm lying in bed looking at the all too familiar walls of my childhood room. As I gaze into my dresser mirror,

I'm stunned, for I'm not sure who is looking back at me.

My mind travels back to October 28. The first day I arrived at MD Anderson Cancer Center in Houston. I remember walking down the halls, seeing all the sick patients. How surreal it all seemed at the time, and how shocked people were when I told them I was sick.

As I glance back into the mirror, I now know where that face belongs—in the halls of Houston.

I comfort myself with what every mother tells their child: "It's not what's on the outside that counts but what's on the inside." The *soul*—something disease can never destroy.

As I lie on my pillow wet with tears, I hear a bird outside my window. It sounds so beautiful. I always love to hear the birds in the morning. As my mind races over the weakness of my body and another five more treatments, I feel like my family has become the coach, and I'm the boxer. Everyone keeps shouting, urging me to get back in the ring, but I can't go. I'm weak, tired, and my immune system has found another body.

As I plead with God, I keep hearing the bird sing. It's as if it is answering my pleas.

Then I recall, "Look at the birds of the air; they do not sow or reap or store away in barns, and yet your heavenly Father feeds them. Are you not much more valuable than they? Who of you by worrying can add a single hour to his life?" (Matthew 6:26–27).

I sit up and try to see the bird, but I can't.

I feel *peace*. I will not worry about another treatment,

but I will focus on today. I will regain strength and enjoy the beauty of this day.

Thank You, God, for sending a bird my way. What a beautiful reminder of my heavenly Father—His presence is powerful even though unseen.

14

Suddenly

Outside the season is changing. Inside, I also see the hope of spring.

March 21

The first day of spring . How to describe it?

Suddenly.

"*Suddenly* my sheaf rose and stood upright..."

"*Suddenly* a great company of the heavenly host appeared..."

"*Suddenly* a light from heaven flashed around him..."

Suddenly the sun shone through the blinds, and I realized I had slept through the night. It was like the morning after your baby sleeps through the night for the first time—minus the panic.

Suddenly I felt renewed strength and energy.

Suddenly I opened the blinds to a beautiful day.

Suddenly I noticed the forsythia was blooming!

I enjoyed breakfast with my mother, and *suddenly* I glanced on the freshly cut jonquils on the table.

Suddenly the phone rang, and it was a college friend I hadn't heard from in twelve years.

Suddenly the doorbell rang, and it was the postal carrier with a package for *me*! Wrapped with a purple bow, it was a gift from my high school buddies.

Suddenly I looked in the mirror and saw a little hair sprouting out on top of my head. For the first time in my life, I could count the number of hairs on my head!

Suddenly the door bell rang again, and a beautiful bouquet of spring flowers laced with purple blooms had arrived. The card had *my* name on it.

After *six* days of being inside, I went out into my parents' yard, and *suddenly* fresh air filled my lungs and my being.

Suddenly I was leaving the Western North Carolina Cancer Center and had completed my twentieth treatment!

It is the first day of *spring*!

As I enjoyed a beautiful Good Friday, I once more noticed the crocuses in my mother's yard planted there by my grandmother. It prompted a message with these words:

To my partners in prayer:

Thank you for planting *seeds* of healing in my life through your prayers. May this Easter bring new beginnings in all our lives.

Easter at Home

Easter is a season of hope. I was finally home in Virginia. I wrote my church family an email.

March 27

Dear Church Family,

God gave me a word today. But I did not speak it. I, like many of you, left church today feeling convicted, and I told myself not to worry about it. But God is a God of second chances, and, while today I didn't meet His best, I came straight home and decided that I would not let the sun set without fulfilling what God had asked me to do.

It started this morning after Stan and the boys left for church. God gave me an analogy that I needed to share, so I called Stan, but no one answered the phone. I thought I would tell him so he could share it with the church. I even tried to call again at 10:55 a.m. Talk about calling it close. At 11:35 a.m., I knew I had to go to church.

In thirty-four years I had never been any place else on Easter Sunday. The problem—I am not supposed to be around people because my blood counts are too low, and on Easter Sunday the church is packed. Moreover, I'm not even dressed for Easter. I put on a green hat and went anyway.

It was the first time I had been in a worship service since October. I was overcome with emotion when I walked in the door.

Then I heard God's still, quiet voice telling me I needed to speak. How is this possible? I'm in the vestibule. How will I get up front? I haven't even discussed this with Stan. What will everyone think? I don't want to draw attention to myself. My voice is weak. I don't even have anything written.

Sound familiar?

Friday we had a birthday party for Briggs at my mom and dad's house. I was so excited and blessed to be feeling the best I'd felt in a month. Due to the medical expense we had incurred this year, I didn't think we should be spending a lot of money on birthday gifts. However, being a mom, and a sick one at that, I wanted to give Briggs something that was special.

A month ago on the plane ride to Houston, a certain person sat behind us. It was Brad Daugherty. For those of you who don't know, he's a basketball player. He played for the University of North Carolina and then went on to play for the Cleveland Cavaliers. Now, he's a sports announcer on ESPN. I decided I would get his autograph. So as we exited the plane I approached him for conversation, much to my husband's disapproval. I've always been the outgoing type. It just happened that I had a blank sheet of white paper in my purse. Much to my delight, he obliged.

When we returned home, Stan started looking through his old basketball cards and found an old Brad Daugherty card. Last week I got the idea to put the card and autograph in a frame I found at Mom and Dad's house. I wrapped it up for Briggs.

Finally, it was time to open presents. I was like a kid—hoping Briggs would love what his mommy had for him. He was ecstatic. I was elated.

When the party was over and all the cousins had left, Briggs came up to me, put his arms around me, and said, "Mom, this is the best gift ever!" He even went to bed with it right beside him.

My point—it was free. I didn't spend a dime.

As I looked around at church this morning, I was brokenhearted at those who live this life valuing only the things they can buy—the fancy cars, houses, etc. We think it makes us feel important. Therefore, we conclude that if it is expensive, it has value in our lives. We go to church and think there's nothing to it—accepting Christ. It's too easy. It's free. Therefore, we conclude that it has no value. We don't need it.

The beauty of Briggs's gift is that he doesn't realize it was free. He's still too young to place a value on what costs the most.

When in life did we quit realizing that the greatest things in life are free?

I'm sending an email. It's my way of making right what I should have said in person.

What did God place on your heart this Easter morning that you didn't do? Don't let the sun set.

Susan

March 28

My twenty-first treatment. My neutrophil blood count is .98, and once again Glenn starts to sniffle and cough. I don't know if he has allergies or a cold, but I can't risk it. I have to fly to Houston in three days. I'm completely distraught.

I decide I will wait until tomorrow to go back to North Carolina. I'm just tired and I know Stan's exhausted. I want to spend some more time with the kids.

I put on a mask. Tonight Stan has a meeting, and I'm alone with the kids. I try to keep my distance from Glenn. His little nose running, he looks up at me and asks, "Mommy, play with me." It's like a dagger stuck into my heart. I can't. It's too risky.

God, please protect my children. Help them understand how deeply I love them both and that my time away from them and my inability to be the mom they need at this moment in their lives is only because I am desperately seeking to heal my body so I can be their mother for a long time.

Joys of the journey—spending the night in my own bed. After three weeks away, it's comforting to be in my own room.

March 29

How thankful I am for good friends and family. Tonight I am at Mom and Dad's. Glenn once more tugged at my heart as he cried for me on the phone.

After five months, I can tell it has taken a toll on the boys. How I long to spend time with them.

March 30

Briggs's birthday. What wonderful memories I have of him being born. How I wish I could be with him today. I left him a card and his photo album from when he was born on the dining room table. I thought he would enjoy it.

As I sat here saying "Poor me," I received a powerful email from the mother of a child who had just died from cancer. May God grant this mother peace and comfort in a way that's possible only by the Holy Spirit. I pray that God will use little Coulten's life to touch others in a remarkable way. That all things would work together for the good of those who love Him. May the testimony of this mother touch us all that we might refocus the kaleidoscope.

Uncertainty at a Crossroads

Once again, I'm in Texas:

April 1

Our meeting with the doctors went well. They were pleased with my progress. They wanted to wait until I completed my last round of treatments before any additional testing was done.

As I write this, MD Anderson just released the following information regarding the clinical trial and treatment plan I am participating in:

"Results show that we can potentially change the natural history of a disease that is associated with a high risk of recurrence and death."

Utterly amazing!

My team of doctors has outlined several surgical options. Praying for wisdom and discernment as I make this important decision.

April 1, evening

Today all intellect and knowledge have failed me. During the past five months I have read every book I know of and have spent hours studying in the library at MD Anderson in Houston. My goal was to become as informed and educated as possible about the disease that has invaded my body. I thought the information and knowledge would eventually direct me to make the best conclusion concerning my health and surgery decision. I am grateful for the information I have obtained and for the doctors who have assisted me in the process.

I find myself at a crossroads, and not even the doctor can tell me which road to take. I continue to review the facts and statistics in my mind. However, they do not direct me to a certain path.

Why does it seem that in the critical decisions in life there are always A and B answers? I have decided the answer to that question must be by design to allow us to focus on the spiritual side of life, and that our faith in God must guide us.

As I wrestle with this decision, I feel empathy toward

all who are faced with medical choices of uncertainty. I remember what a dear lady in my church told me at the beginning of this journey: "While you've been talking to the doctors, we've been talking to God." How profound it seemed the instant she spoke it, and how it rings in my inner being today.

I am so thankful for all the individuals who are praying for me. The power of those prayers continues to utterly amaze me.

April 2

Dr. R. still had not received my MRI reports that I had sent from Duke. Getting your own film is an unbelievable process. It took me a month to get Duke to release the film to Houston. Duke shows it was sent and signed for. But somehow when it got to Houston, the film got lost! Here we are to make surgery preparations, and I don't have it.

Dr. R. assured me there was nothing on the film that would change his mind. I wanted to believe him, but something inside me keeps telling me I need that film.

All day Stan and I comb this hospital trying to find someone who might know where the film ended up.

Tonight Stan gets a call from my oncologist. He has found the film in his office. He hand-delivers the film to Stan in the hotel restaurant. Tomorrow morning we will hand-deliver it to Dr. R. before we fly back to North Carolina.

15

Decisions

I had heavy decisions to make. Mastectomy or lumpectomy? Reconstruction or not?

I was learning that it was my responsibility to search for the missing pieces in my medical puzzle.

April 4

The surgeon suggests that I have a lumpectomy and radiation, since my tumors have responded so well to the chemo.

I have read and read over the two options. Mastectomy or lumpectomy? It's constantly on my mind. What if I make the wrong choice?

Obviously a lumpectomy would be the easiest in terms of emotions, surgery, and time of healing. But if the cancer came back, would I always regret not having a mastectomy?

I have also consulted with doctors at Johns Hopkins. Everyone says that whether you choose a mastectomy or lumpectomy does not dictate whether your cancer will return. According to all the research I have found and discussed with doctors, having a mastectomy will reduce my chance of recurrence by only about 8 percent. The doctors also have cautioned me that just because I have a mastectomy doesn't mean the cancer can't return in that breast. The fact is they can't and don't remove all the breast tissue. Dr. R. shared with me about a patient who had a mastectomy whose breast cancer returned in the same breast. He assures me that he is more worried about cancer recurring somewhere else in my body than in my breast.

So back to teeter-tottering. Mastectomy or lumpectomy? The more I read, the more science seems to suggest a lumpectomy.

I search message boards and read about different women's experiences. I talk with cancer survivors from MD Anderson about the choice they made and how they made it.

I have to give Dr. R. an answer in a week, because he will need to schedule my surgery, and depending on the option I choose, it will greatly alter what is needed at the time of surgery.

If I choose mastectomy, will I reconstruct? If so, there are so many options for reconstruction. Which one should I choose?

Endless medical decisions.

I keep praying that God will show me what to do. I am not afraid of losing a breast, although I know there will be emotional issues to follow. I just want to live and live to the fullest.

Mastectomy will be painful. Not just the surgery but more so the reconstruction. Everyone I have talked with noted the pain of reconstruction. Stan and I talk over the issue, and he wants it to be *my* decision.

April 7

I am back in my parents' home in North Carolina. I am down to the wire. I don't know what to do. I decide to take the surgeon's recommendation and have a lumpectomy. If at the time of surgery he feels I should go ahead and have a mastectomy, then we will take that action.

I call his nurse to schedule the surgery and let her know my decision.

A New Concern

The day after my decision, I received a call from Dr. R.'s PA. She stated that Dr. R. had received the MRI from Duke. He had reviewed it with the best radiologist on staff at MD Anderson. There *was* something on the film, and it concerned them. With this information, Dr. R. felt a mastectomy was the best surgical option.

She scheduled the surgery for May 18, and told me Dr. R. would schedule me to see a plastic surgeon so we could do the reconstruction at the same time.

I hung up the phone and felt sick. I ran into my room, fell on my bed, and began to cry. As tears streamed down my face, I felt a flurry of emotions—from "Praise the Lord for His care for me" to "I don't want to lose my breast" to "If there was cancer hiding there, where else might it be that no one saw?"

I called Stan, and he tried to encourage me that this was God answering our prayers. I knew he was right.

I got up, collected myself, and went downstairs to tell my parents.

That night as I lay in bed, I thought of what had transpired during the past six months. I recalled how God had used all my medical experiences to lead me where I was today. How the Houston doctors had told me they were 99 percent sure the tumor was not attached. How I decided to go back to Duke anyway to have an MRI, and to try to put the final pieces to the puzzle of where I should receive treatment. Houston had been right—the tumor wasn't attached. But the Duke MRI was needed to lead me where I was today.

That was why I couldn't feel confirmation from God. I felt so much pressure from the world and from everyone to decide—but God had a plan I couldn't have understood at that moment. And, in the eleventh hour, I did know that God was leading me to Houston. But this experience had to come first. Yes, buying plane tickets the night before you fly is expensive, but imagine the cost of a wrong medical decision.

Lying in the hospital in Asheville sick with a neutropenic fever in February, my mind had gone back to October's MRI. I'd felt it could be a missing piece to my medical puzzle. I believed God was and is guiding me.

"Lord, You don't promise me a life void of pain, but You do promise me one that is utterly amazing. When I ponder the events of this day, I feel Your presence right here beside me. Your favor is on my shoulders. May all creatures in heaven and earth praise the Lord."

Praise be to the name of God for ever and ever;
Wisdom and power are his. He changes times and
seasons; He sets up kings and deposes them; He gives
wisdom to the wise and knowledge to the discerning.
He reveals deep and hidden things; He knows what
lies in the darkness, and light dwells with him. (Daniel
2:20–22)

A New Prayer

I began to recall Dr. R. telling me that this would be a very painful
surgery. The surgery and reconstruction would be complicated, and
only a handful of doctors in the country had performed it. I began
researching the options he had shared with me. As I did, my prayer
changed to: "Lord, help me find the right doctor for this procedure."

April 18

Today I took my twenty-fourth treatment. I did
it! What seemed impossible in November is now
completed.

My body is so tired and frail. I wonder in my mind if
I will ever recover. I know hair will grow back. I don't
know if the neuropathy in my hands and feet will ever
leave, but today I don't care. I did it, and just like the
boy who didn't miss giving out a single valentine to his
classmates, I didn't miss a treatment.

May 5

Fasten your seatbelt as we prepare for takeoff. It's 6:30
a.m. in Asheville, North Carolina. What a declaration
it was for the beginning of this day.

It's Stan's seventeenth flight since October. Talk about facing your fears! That boy deserves a prize when this journey is through.

Wonderful flight, and we're en route to MD Anderson Cancer Center.

I'm sitting in the waiting room awaiting my visit with the surgeon. I'm appalled over the magazine selection covered with scantily clothed women and bathing-suit styles for summer . Who would think this is appropriate reading for a room full of breast-cancer patients? Laying nearby is a handbook graphically showing how they are going to cut, slice, and maim your body to rid you of this life-threatening disease.

Stan and I decide to laugh abruptly. How else can you react to the actions of some well-meaning soul?

I felt like I was on a jet moving at lightning speed as I met with three different doctors at different places in the hospital while also having other tests done. Going from place to place wasn't the difficult part. However, trying to absorb all the information while formulating fact-finding questions is completely draining, especially for someone who does not like to look at people's battle wounds, much less think of their own.

I concluded today that Daddy was right when he warned, "They're going to cut you up like a jigsaw puzzle."

Oh, well, I concluded that some jigsaw puzzles when put together make beautiful art!

Not only did God grant us a wonderful flight, but

we were able to meet with all the doctors whom we wanted to see, and each gave us attentive and ample time. I attribute these continued miracles in my life to the many individuals who so diligently pray for me.

It's 11:30 p.m., and I'm calling it a day. Just as our seatbelt protects us at times of collision, so does our heavenly Father when life collides with the unexpected.

May God grant me infinite wisdom and peace as I make final health decisions.

May 8, Mother's Day

Today I can't help but think of all the women who have played intricate roles in my life. They have all mothered me in different ways, yet the most transforming has been through the power of their prayers. I have come to understand that we can't fully comprehend the power of prayer until we experience it.

Lord, thank You that You know my name and You hear me when I call.

May 16

Today my surgeon returned my call, and we talked for forty-five minutes.

After our conversation, I felt peace, and I was awestruck at the power and care of Almighty God. I feel so loved by my heavenly Father. Knowing that He cares about my every need and desire.

I realize that my difficulty in making a decision stems from fear—I am so fearful that I will make the wrong one.

Trust and faith. God's faithfulness during this journey has been unfathomable to me.

God must be tired of me coming to Him with my list of requests, but He is the Healer, and He says to "fear not." May His favor rest upon me in a powerful way.

Lord, tonight I pray for healing for Paula, Chris, and Karen. Friends who are all going through cancer treatment and are struggling.

Paula, Chris, and Karen have all gone on to be with the Lord. Their earthly life was brief, but the impact that each of them had on my heart was enormous.

16

Goodbye

Surgery is different from chemo. In chemo, they're putting something into you. In surgery, they're taking something away.

May 17

> During my pre-op, the nurse instructed me not to use mousse or hairspray tomorrow! What hair?
>
> The doctor asked me during our consultation today if I worked in the medical field. Amid Stan's abrupt laughter, I answered, "No, I am a banker." After thinking on that question tonight, I believe I could be a patient advocate after my experience as a patient.
>
> Peace—what an overwhelming gift and provision from God. Tonight I have peace about the surgery decisions I have made.
>
> Though the answer lingers, it always comes.
>
> "Though it linger, wait for it, it will certainly come and will not delay" (Habakkuk 2:3).

I have learned while we wait, we must earnestly seek God and information, and in His timing we will know.

Tonight I said goodbye to the body I have known.

Provisions

Stan and I sent the following email to our church family and friends.

May 17

"Take provisions for your journey" (Joshua 9:11).

Thank you for being instrumental in the provisions for my journey. Tonight God has given me the provision of *peace*.

"Peace I leave with you; my peace I give you. I do not give to you as the world gives. Do not let your hearts be troubled and do not be afraid" (John 14:27).

It is breathtaking to think of the love and prayer support you have blanketed me with. Tomorrow should be an easy day for me as I will be asleep for most of it. Please pray for Stan and my mom, as I know that waiting all day will be tense and exhausting.

Love,

Susan

Dear Church Family,

Thank you for your committed prayers for Susan. She is trying to recover from a difficult surgery. The surgery lasted a little over eight hours. Overall, she did pretty good. She has been sick for the last two days, evidently from a combination of prolonged anesthesia and medication. She is really sore, but that was expected. Please pray that she will be on her feet soon.

Praise and Prayer:

The surgeon said that the tentative test results show no lymph node involvement. That was great news. This was only an initial test. Her surgeon said to be positive, but patiently wait on the final results. Please continue to pray that the final pathology reports next week confirm that the initial results are correct.

Also, the tumors had been greatly impacted by all the chemo. But we will not know until next week the results of the tests on those. Please pray that they were cancer free.

God is good. And we praise Him daily for answered prayers and a wonderful church family.

God bless, and I hope to see you all soon.

Stan

Not One Bad Cell

Following the surgery I was unable to write in my journal. I dictated the following journal entry to Stan.

May 24

Today, Dr. R. came by to give us the pathology report.

Lymph nodes are cancer free.

All tissue removed showed no invasive cancer remaining.

And God answered *our* prayers: "not one bad cell."

"Look at the nations and watch—and be utterly amazed. For I am going to do something in your day that you would not believe even if you were told" (Habakkuk 1:5).

And my husband sent this message:

> Susan remains in the hospital. She is slowly recovering from her lengthy surgery. The doctors expect her to remain in the hospital several more days. Please continue to pray for her.
>
> Thanks for being our prayer partners.
>
> God Bless,
>
> Stan

17

The Other Side of Surgery

It's okay to cry, and it's okay to let those you love cry.

When people we love are upset, we tend to want to help them respond differently. If that doesn't work, then we try the drill-sergeant approach. My family's favorite: "Let's not shed any tears or have anyone upset."

We all know that grieving is healthy—we just don't want anyone to do it. It makes us feel bad and helpless. As if we had the power to heal someone's pain.

I was upset about my surgery decisions. I was having significant pain—and so far pain pills (narcotics) and me had not been having a happy relationship.

Then there were the horrifying scars and drain tubes coming out of every side of my torso.

Hearing My Shepherd

On this day, in my sorrow, I decided I needed no assistance. So I climbed out of bed and walked down the hall, slumped over and holding onto my IV stand. As I walked around the nurse's station, I passed the room of a terminally ill patient. Someone was sitting by the bed reading Psalm 23. "The LORD is my shepherd…" I stood there for a moment just to hear God's Word. Jesus and His Word is all you need in times of suffering.

I'd also learned that there's power in *touch*. I'd heard individuals say prayers from time to time that were so powerful I felt they came straight from God. A few nights earlier, as I cried, a nurse had come in and touched me, and that touch felt like it came straight from heaven. That woman is gifted with the power of touch, and when she touches you, you feel comfort. She said "Peace," and rubbed my arm. Then she began to whisper over and over, "Jesus, give her peace."

Something else I'd learned is that if you will sit still and listen to others, it's amazing what you can learn.

On this day, Stan decided it was time for me to get out of my cramped hospital room. He wheeled me to the atrium to listen to someone playing the grand piano. Mentally, it did me so much good to get out of my room.

As I gazed over my apparel, I couldn't decide if I looked more like a homeless person or a bag lady. My attire centered on a chic unisex hospital gown that gave the appearance of having been through at least a couple thousand wash cycles. Tightly covering my feet and legs were the stark white hospital stockings, plus worn-out leopard-print slippers. Wrapped around my shoulders was a mint-green robe. My head was cutely adorned with a crocheted multicolored cap that one of the hospital volunteers had made for me. My lap held my pillow—red on one side and navy with red tulips on the other.

Where's a camera when you need one?

May 25

Today Briggs will have his first two teeth pulled. Tonight the tooth fairy will come to the Parris household for the first time. I never imagined missing these events in my children's lives, but today I rejoice that the next time I see the boys, Briggs and I will both be sporting new looks!

Today I am being released from the hospital after a seven-night stay. We will be staying at the Rotary House until I am able to travel back home.

It is still painful for me to view the scars on my body.

It has been exactly one week since my surgery.

May 27

I receive pink roses from friends. What a bright spot in my day.

May 28

Stan left for North Carolina. It will be fourteen days tomorrow since leaving the boys. Briggs and Glenn are both sick, and we are anxious for Stan to get home to them. They both want to know why Mommy isn't coming with him.

I am forever indebted to my in-laws, Jerry and JoAnne, for taking such good care of the boys in our absence.

May 30

Memorial Day. After thirteen days of being indoors, I put on real clothes for the first time, and Mom wheels me outdoors. It's a warm Houston day with a refreshing breeze. The aroma of flowers fills the air, and a bird flies down to the bench beside me. He looks at me as if to say hello. I watch another bird dive into a bird bath, spinning around in the water and flying away, seemingly refreshed.

"This is the day that the Lord has given, we shall be glad and rejoice in it." (Psalm 118:24 TLB)

June 2

As I wheeled myself out of my room, onto the elevator, and then outside, I begin to have a whole new respect for individuals who depend on a wheelchair for mobility. It's a good thing I'm in Texas where it's flat—it takes a lot of upper-body strength to get a wheelchair up an incline. Likewise, it's also difficult going down.

I sat outside enjoying the sunshine, reflecting on what life is like for the physically impaired.

Another Mountain to Climb

As I met with the surgeon and oncologist, I was anticipating my release with the exception of follow-up visits. In the waiting room, I mentally planned my summer and looked forward to having the CVC line removed from my chest.

We enjoyed our usual pleasant exchanges, and then Dr. R. gave me a huge hug and high five. He and Dr. T. were obviously excited about my pathology findings and rightfully so. They were *utterly amazing!*

It was what they recommended next that caught me off

guard—six more months of treatment! I was sure I'd misunderstood, for this had never before been mentioned. They discussed my particular type of cancer and how aggressive it is and the high recurrence rate associated with it—all of which I already knew. Next, Dr. T. discussed some new information just released on a study about women with my type of cancer. It showed that I could reduce my risk of recurrence by 50 percent, if I took the additional six months of treatment.

I asked him when I would need to start, and he responded, "Next week."

Again I was sure I hadn't heard him correctly.

"On the positive side," he commented, "it will only be every three weeks, and you'll be done by Christmas."

My mind began to wander to the story of Joseph in Genesis—how he was promised release from prison, only to spend another two years there. But Joseph's life didn't end in prison. Instead he went on to live an amazing and abundant life.

I've found that sometimes, when you get to the top of the mountain, another one appears behind it.

June 3

Disappointed? Yes. Defeated? No.

June 4

Today is my birthday. I am thirty-five years old. Mom wakes up this morning and wishes me a happy birthday. I don't want to think about it being my birthday today. I am grateful to be alive and another year older, but birthday wishes I can do without.

I never imagined my body would look like this at

thirty-five. I glance at myself a long time in the mirror. My hair is beginning to come back in places. It feels like baby hair. So soft.

I do a heparin flush on the CVC line inserted in my chest. I thought I would be taking a shower today for the first time since October. Instead, these tubes are still attached.

Back in the bathtub I crawl. It will be six more months before I feel water spray over my body and face in a shower.

A Fallen Rearview Mirror

Looking out the window at the beautiful Texas sky, I was reminded of an afternoon nine years earlier. Stan and I were living in Fort Worth. It was August 1995, and the Texas heat was unbearable. As I left my office at the bank that hot afternoon, I was startled when I opened my car door. Laying on the floorboard was my rearview mirror. The heat had melted the glue holding the mirror to the glass. I was facing afternoon rush hour without a rearview mirror. What timing! I recall telling myself to fasten my seat belt, say a prayer, take hold of the hand of God, and move ahead. By the grace of God I made it home through rush-hour traffic. Stan and I laughed about the incident at the time, then forgot about it.

But on this afternoon I thought of it again. I realized God was giving me an object lesson that would be pivotal to my mental health.

Maybe there are times in life you need to let the rearview mirror fall to the floorboard. It's natural to think about what could have been. What if the doctors had diagnosed me correctly the first time? How different would my life be today? How different would my life be long-term?

Sometimes seeing life through the rearview mirror is unproductive, painful, and paralyzing. I didn't want to focus on the rearview mirror and miss what was happening in front of me.

Being misdiagnosed was a rearview-mirror moment. I'd learned from it—and I decided I eventually wanted to help and educate others so they would never have the same experience.

One cannot live life thinking about what could have been. *Lord, I prayed, let this rearview mirror fall to the floor. May I take hold of the hand of God and move forward, trusting His sovereignty.*

June 4

Mom and I will fly back to North Carolina today. How grateful I am that she has been here with me in Texas for *three* weeks. I know it has been exhausting for her. There are times in life when a mother's care is priceless…no matter how old you are.

The surgery phase is over and I have survived. I put on my same black hat and wait for our taxi to come and take us to the airport.

Today I will be ushered through the airport in a wheelchair. I am not strong enough to do much walking yet. It's so humbling to have someone push you in a wheelchair. People glancing at you as you pass by. I just want to stand up, put on a wig, and look normal.

The "well world" is so superficial and cruel. The "sick world" is refreshingly loving and compassionate—fragile yet resilient. In the sick world, the human spirit is accepting of all kinds, never judgmental, seeing people for who they really are, and celebrating that life.

June 6

Home sweet home. Stan has rushed to North Carolina on this Monday morning to pick me up and usher me back to Virginia.

The four-hour drive seems like eternity today. It is a huge day. I am so excited and filled with emotion. Briggs will graduate from kindergarten. I can't even say the words without welling up in tears. He will wear his Easter outfit. Seersucker pants, white polo shirt, and vest.

As we drive, I visualize the event in my mind. It has been one of my goals for months—to be present at Briggs's kindergarten graduation and to *walk* into the auditorium.

After being in a wheelchair for the past several weeks, I am determined tonight I will walk from the front door of the school into the gymnasium. I will stand tall and appear healthy and well for my son.

Pride fills every fiber of my being as I watch him march in with his class. It is the first time I have been at his school since October. I watch the children glance at me and my straw hat. I hope he is not embarrassed.

Glenn sits close beside me as Tami and Stan take pictures. His entire kindergarten year has been a blur to me. I feel so detached from his world and his friends. Like a stranger in my own small town.

I am so emotional I have to fight back tears. How blessed I am to be here.

June 18

Karen is dead. Her battle with breast cancer is over. At forty years of age she leaves behind a loving husband and two children. A dedicated Christian—I know she is now in heaven. I am deeply saddened for her family. I feel numb. What is it like to lie in a bed dying, yet know that your children need you?

What a dreadful disease—a silent killer. Invading your body without warning.

June 19

I hear my daddy's voice, "Susan, quit blowing those dandelions in the yard. They just take seed and multiply. We don't want those old dandelions in our yard." So often as a child, I would blow the dandelions when Daddy wasn't watching. I thought they were beautiful floating through the air.

Today, I closed my eyes and blew a dandelion in our yard. I envisioned God blowing healthy cells throughout my body. Cells that would multiply and not fail.

June 21

Picture day! The kids and I venture to the department of motor vehicles (DMV) to renew my license. At thirty-five years of age I have obviously been through the process before, but my chemo brain failed to remember what was required. First, an eye test. Oops! I just thought I was coming in here to pay a fee and leave with a new license. I didn't even bring my glasses, and my eyesight has worsened over the past year. I adjust my eyes as I look into the binocular-type machine. *Focus*, Susan. Concentrate. Strain. For goodness sake, you don't want to have your picture remade! I recall how that used to be the punishment if you failed the eye exam.

Whew—it appears I passed. What a relief.

They ask if I would want my picture remade. I quickly respond, "No."

Seeing that I'm wearing a turban and a hat on my head, I much prefer the picture I already have—with flowing locks of dark brown hair and a much younger-looking face.

Next the shocker: "Mrs. Parris, your picture has expired. We have to take a new one."

Ouch.

As I look at my new license, two things come to mind. First, how a picture can starkly remind us of what we really look like. Second, at least when I go through airport security, they won't have to stare at my driver's license to determine if it's really me!

June 24

Tonight as I tuck Briggs into bed, he begs to stay up longer. We have the usual conversation of why going to bed is good for you and your body needs rest, not very convincing to a six year old.

As I continue to babble, his countenance changes. He interrupts my monologue. "Do you know why I don't want to go to sleep?" Before I can respond, he answers his own question. "I am afraid I will have a bad dream." I am caught off guard. I thought he just wanted to stay up and play. His now penetrating eyes focus on my face. I lie down beside him.

Stan had told me Briggs had been having bad dreams for several months. He would wake up in the middle of the night claiming to have had a bad dream, but could never tell anyone what the dream was about. Always stating he couldn't remember. We didn't think it was too unusual. Other parents said their kids did the same thing.

Lying side by side, he continued to open up. "Mommy, do you know what happens in my bad dreams?"

"No, son, I do not."

"I always dream the same thing. I dream you go to Texas and you never come back."

I wrap my arms around him. My heart wants to tell him I will always come back. Isn't that what parents are supposed to say? Then my mind races to Karen. That is what she told her children, and then she didn't come back. I recall her husband saying how angry their son was because his mom had promised she would come back. Karen planned on coming back—but her body began to fail, and she went into cardiac arrest and died.

I feel like a dagger just went through my heart. I don't want my family to have any more pain. I want to cry streams of tears. Instead I turn over and look Briggs right in the eye.

"Briggs, you never have to be afraid. God tells us in the Bible, '*Fear not*. I am with you.' No matter where I am, God is with me. He is right here with you too. One promise I can make you, when you ask Jesus to come into your heart, He will always be with you. Forever."

We closed our eyes and said a prayer together, thanking God that He was right there beside us.

June 26

I have officially reentered the "well world." This afternoon I went to the grocery store for the first time since October. I was actually excited about embarking on this mundane task. What new and exciting products have they introduced during my absence?

After entering the store, I immediately realized that everything had been rearranged. What used to be on aisle two was no longer on aisle two, and where in the world were the raisins and canned fruit? As I navigated down each aisle straining to read the signs overhead, the products it contained, it occurred to me: "This is what it must feel like to be a man!"

As I left the store, I realized I had enjoyed this typically dreaded family task. I was glad my grocery store had changed. Not only had it changed the arrangements of the products inside, but they had new colored bags into which they placed my groceries.

Like my grocery store, I too have changed. My packaging is a little different. But in no time it will all seem like old hat—and so it will be with my body.

June 29

Today was my day to feel like a woman again. I went to the salon and had my neck shaved and the sparsely scattered eyebrows tweaked. What a wonderful feeling to be pampered and feel like I'm functioning in the world I once loved.

It's been six weeks since my surgery, and I'm feeling better than I thought I would at this point. Just being back in the "well world" again with my children and friends has made my body and mind thrive. Oh—and my hair too!

June 30

To my partners in prayer:

I hope this email finds you well and enjoying the summer sun!

I will travel to North Carolina on Sunday afternoon. Staying with tradition, our family will enjoy July 4th in Waynesville. On Tuesday, I will take another treatment. Thank you for the prayers uplifted for my continued restored health.

Celebrating,

Susan

18

From Tranquility to Crisis to Hope

The story of Job is one of the most famous stories in the Bible. Yet, despite its fame, there are a lot of questions about the book of Job. No one knows who wrote it. No one knows where it was written. I think that's God's design. The book is universal. It's for all of us.

Job is a book of questions—more than 300 of them in its forty-two chapters. In fact, Job asks the question "Why?" more than twenty times.

God never answered that question for Job.

We often ask why. *Why did my business fail? Why did I lose my house? Why did my spouse leave me? Why do I have cancer?* Solomon said, "For with much wisdom comes much sorrow; the more knowledge, the more grief" (Ecclesiastes 1:18). God teaches us that if you know the answer, you'll grieve even more. In other words, knowledge increases pain. The blessing and grace of God is that He does not tell us why.

Job, according to God's testimony, was blameless and upright. In fact, if you're looking for a deserving candidate for suffering, Job doesn't seem to be an appropriate one. He was known for his reverence to God, and in fact one translation of the Bible speaks of Job as being "perfect." *Perfect* doesn't mean without sin; its real meaning in this verse is "whole," as opposed to being fractured. Job's allegiance to God was not divided. He feared God.

Job was also blessed. He had seven sons and three daughters. (Seven and three are the most significant symbolic numbers in the Bible, both with complex connotations of wholeness and completeness.) God's favor rested on Job. He had sheep, camels, oxen and servants. In fact, the Bible says he was the greatest man in all the East. God had blessed Job.

Life for Job was great. The family was celebrating life to its fullest, as we quickly see in the book:

> His sons used to take turns holding feasts in their homes, and they would invite their three sisters to eat and drink with them. When a period of feasting had run its course, Job would send and have them purified. Early in the morning he would sacrifice a burnt offering for each of them, thinking, "Perhaps my children have sinned and cursed God in their hearts." (Job 1:4–5)

This was Job's regular custom. The family was celebrating—and Job was confessing.

All was well in the Job residence. If Job only knew how much would change so soon!

We experience this story from a totally different perspective than Job. He had no clue about what was happening behind the scenes. Job never saw it coming—and God never explained it to him.

I arrived in Waynesville for our Fourth of July celebration, one of my favorite times of the year: fireworks, family, homemade ice cream, and twenty-four-hour Andy Griffith marathons on television. Independence Day is a great time for me and my family because of several traditions that are always a part of the celebration. Freedom is a reason to celebrate.

This day follows a traditional schedule for the Parris family. We start the morning with the parade at Lake Junaluska. The parade is simple, patriotic, and sometimes silly. But being there for it is a tradition that unites our family together each year. The boys dress in their patriotic colors and carry their small American flags. They also bring along a plastic bag to catch all the candy thrown during the parade.

For this year, Mom bought me a straw hat. I wrapped a red, white, and blue scarf around it to cover my bald head and joined in on the patriotic spirit.

The fire engines, tractors, and old-timers band were a familiar sight, in addition to entire families walking the parade route. The lifeguards from the swimming pool kept up their tiring tradition of squirting the crowd with water from their squirt guns. When the boys were really little, this annual annoyance had brought about fear and trepidation to the point that Stan was ready to break those plastic guns over the lifeguards' heads. Thankfully, this year God smiled on the Parris family, and we all remained dry and calm!

Following the parade, we spent the day with family and friends. Stan's family gathered for a cookout at his parents' house with his aunts, uncles, and cousins. The boys got to see and play with their cousins, a special treat. Later we joined with my family for another cookout with some long-time friends.

As always, the day ended back at Lake Junaluska with the annual fireworks.

The familiar sights and sounds of the day reminded me again that despite all the changes in my life, God does not change—and neither do His promises to me.

As I basked in the joy of that time, I was unaware that just around the corner, my life would take another unexpected turn. I'll never know the exact details of what happened, but somehow my youngest son, Glenn, came close to losing his life on the farm I so deeply cherish.

King Solomon was right: "No man knows when his hour will come: As fish are caught in a cruel net, or birds are taken in a snare, so men are trapped by evil times that fall *unexpectedly* upon them" (Ecclesiastes 9:12).

Unexpected Turn

Stan was back in Virginia preparing for the Sunday worship service. The boys and I were enjoying a few days on the farm with my parents. My brother, Brian, had decided to take the boys on a ride down to the bottom fields to check on the cows. He was driving the tractor and pulling behind a fourteen-foot, metal-framed hay trailer. The boys, along with their cousin, Bradley, were riding on the trailer.

All the boys were having fun on the hay trailer, maybe too much fun. Four-year-old Glenn, with his resilient attitude, was determined to keep up with the "big" boys and do everything they were doing, and more.

Glenn attempted to jump off the moving trailer, but his foot didn't clear the edge; it got caught between the edge and the wheel of the trailer. Then the trailer dragged him upside down for several feet and the wheel rolled over his body. Glenn raised his arms to protect himself from the wheel. Then the second set of wheels rolled over his little body of less than forty pounds.

The other boys were screaming, but the tractor was so loud it took several minutes before my brother could hear them. When Brian turned he saw Glenn in the field lying face down. He immediately ran to him. Glenn was trying to get up but couldn't. Brian knew instantly the injuries were serious.

I remember hearing Briggs scream. It was one of those screams that a mother knows instantly—something's bad wrong. I remember Briggs running toward me crying and just repeating Glenn's name over and over, and saying, "He's run over; he's run over." Fear gripped his face. Panic penetrated his hazel eyes. I wanted to assure his frightened voice, to calm him. But then I saw Brian, and, as our eyes met, I too felt panic all around.

Then I saw Glenn. I remember his ears were already turning purple, and his eyes were rolled back. I instantly wanted to know what had happened. Brian didn't offer any explanation; he just told me to get in the car, that we had to get Glenn to the hospital.

I began to feel anger, panic, and fear. I wanted to cry or possibly sob. I looked over at my dad as tears began to fill my eyes. He gave me the best advice: "Susan, now is not the time to get emotional. You need to remain calm, so you can make the best decisions for Glenn." I knew he was right.

I jumped in the back seat with Glenn in my lap and Brian driving. The hospital is only a few miles from my parents' farm. I tried to get Glenn to talk to me but "ahuh" was about all I could get out of him. His little denim shorts were ripped in two and his shirt was torn. I tried to question Brian, "Did you run over him? What happened?" He just responded. "Susan, I didn't run over him. I would have felt the trailer go over him."

That eased my fears as I pulled little pieces of rock and briars from his head.

We rushed into the emergency room. Brian carried Glenn, as I was still recovering from my surgery. When they laid him on the stretcher and began to remove his clothing I saw it. Tire marks across his back. Then the doctor repeated, "He has been run over.

He has been run over." No sooner had those words left the doctor's mouth, than blood began to release from Glenn's body. My medical knowledge is limited, but I knew that was a bad sign.

They immediately rushed him in for a CAT scan. I waited anxiously beside Brian.

The doctor met us in the hallway and told us Glenn was bleeding internally and would need to be transported to a trauma center. He told us he thought Glenn would need immediate surgery to stop the bleeding.

They began preparing Glenn for the ambulance ride. He still hadn't shed the first tear or complained. He calmly lay on the stretcher, his body in shock. The nurse tried to keep him awake and ease his fears by giving him a stuffed bear dressed in red, white, and blue. He took it in his arms. We kept prodding him to give the bear a name. He finally responded in a weak voice, "America." What a moment of relief for me. I was stunned that amid the pain, fear, and complete shock Glenn must have been in, he came up with a great and appropriate name. I knew cognitively he was okay.

Care-Giving 101

My phone began to ring. It was Stan. I dreaded answering this call. I didn't want to tell him what had happened. I hated that such a horrible thing had happened in the care of my family on our farm.

I was very calm, as if to convey an "everything's going to be okay" image through the phone. I had to inform him that Glenn was bleeding internally and we were being transported to the trauma center.

I could instantly hear the concern in Stan's voice. Immediately he moved into the fact-finding analysis mode. I tried to give him all the information the doctor had given me. He jotted everything down. "Call me as soon as you arrive at the trauma center. I'm on my way." I begged him to drive slowly.

It was Saturday night. Stan was supposed to preach the next morning in Virginia. We were almost four hours away from him.

This was my first experience riding in an ambulance. The year was continuing to introduce a lot of firsts to me. I climbed into the back, where the nurse gave me a side seat and instructed me to wear the seat belt. They rolled Glenn on the stretcher into the middle of the ambulance.

Knowing the power of human touch, I was determined to hold his hand the entire trip. I felt exhausted, and my own body was sore. The seat belt tugged across my incision site, but I never let go of Glenn's hand. I just kept talking to him and telling him I loved him, though he never responded or opened his eyes.

His blood pressure kept dropping, and the nurses kept working with him.

I kept praying. Amazingly, I was truly calm. I remember looking down at his little body and purple face, realizing that Glenn didn't belong to me. He belonged to God. He was just in my care for however many days the Lord gave him to me. Just as I'd seen my own immortality, now I was seeing Glenn's.

As I held onto his hand, I just kept praying that God would stop the bleeding in his body. I just kept praying Habakkuk 1:5 over and over—that God would do something utterly amazing in this situation.

They rushed us into the emergency room at the trauma center, where a medical team was waiting for Glenn. I looked on as the doctors examined him and reviewed his test results.

I called Stan, and he immediately began giving me advice. While he was driving, he'd been calling friends to glean information about Glenn's situation. He'd connected with a doctor who recommended a surgeon at the trauma center in case Glenn needed immediate surgery. He also gave Stan a list of questions to ask regarding Glenn's situation. Moving to the investigation stage of the situation was familiar to me, and it helped me remove my emotions and focus on making good informed decisions for Glenn's health.

The emergency room nurse realized Glenn had never been given anything for pain. I didn't realize he was in pain. He was just lying there like he was trying to go to sleep with one arm around his bear, America.

Eventually they moved him into the intensive care unit (ICU). The doctors decided they wanted to monitor the bleeding before they made a decision regarding surgery. By this time, Stan's parents and his brother and sister-in-law had arrived at the hospital. Stan's mom teared up when she saw Glenn.

I hurt for everyone tonight: Glenn, who was so severely injured; Brian, my dear brother, who looked pale and physically sick about the situation; and Stan, who was always rushing to our aid. I couldn't imagine the stress he felt as he drove to be with us.

I was having a mental battle, and I couldn't think about what or how this had happened. I just had to focus on what to do now.

About three o'clock in the morning, Glenn's bleeding stopped. Once again I stood *utterly amazed*. Stan had arrived, and made me go lie down. The nurses let Stan sit beside Glenn all night long in ICU. The strength of that man throughout the past nine months continues to amaze me. How blessed I am to have him as my life-mate.

Pediatric ICU is a sad place, as you look around at the hurt and sick children. Each one is precious.

The doctor who had admitted Glenn came to check on him the next morning. Glenn's recovery was nothing short of unbelievable. Once he was able to be moved to a regular room, he was scheduled to begin physical therapy. Glenn had broken his pelvic bone on both sides and also a bone in his back. The doctors informed us he would be in a wheelchair for two weeks, and would then be using a walker.

The first day the physical therapist came to Glenn's room, she brought a wheelchair. Glenn just looked at her and responded, "I want to walk with my wegs." To our amazement, they put a walker in front of Glenn, and he took a few steps. His determination and resilience in the midst of pain was a remarkable sight. Glenn never used the wheelchair.

After being discharged from the hospital, Glenn continued physical therapy in North Carolina. Every day, my dad would drive us thirty minutes to Asheville for Glenn to have water therapy. At other times, Daddy or Brian would carry Glenn around the house or up the stairs.

Stan went back to Virginia after Glenn was discharged from the hospital. Before he drove away, he said to me, "Susan, I have one family member in chemotherapy and one family member in physical therapy. Can we just lie low? I don't think I can take anything else."

I assured him we would all be as careful as possible.

An hour after Stan had left, Briggs came running up to me and asked, "Mom, can I learn to ride my bike without my training wheels today?"

"Absolutely not!" I quickly answered.

Like a dog with its tail between its legs, Briggs walked back outside and sat on the porch staring at his bike with training wheels. I pondered that picture for a moment, then concluded, *I will not let fear of cancer or fear of an accident control me.*

That day Briggs learned to ride his bike without his training wheels.

Hope from Job

As I reflected on what was happening, it brought to mind the kind of experience Job went through. I recognize that my own life is not like Job's; I'm not comparing my circumstances to his, nor am I pridefully equating my spirituality with Job's. However, I do believe that God can use Job's story to help all of us deal with our dark days.

The book of Job is really about an attack on God. Satan basically tells God, "To get people's worship, You have to bribe them." Satan told God that if He ever took away Job's blessings, Job would curse Him to His face. In other words, Satan was trying to drive a wedge between God and Job.

That's what Satan always does. He uses the same tactics with us. He tries to drive a wedge in our marriage, in our business, in our church, and in our relationship with God.

I was determined that by God's grace these dark days would make my faith stronger, not weaker. God had taken some of the most difficult moments of my life and used them to help me grow close to Him. I was trusting Him more than ever.

What did Job do in the dark days of his life? He grieved. We often miss this part of the story. Job tore his robes and shaved his head, a recognized way in Job's day to express deep, inner sorrow. Job was devastated.

There are those who say that as a Christian, you always have to keep it together. Some even think it's spiritual to never show your emotion. But listen to these words from teacher and pastor John Piper, from his sermon titled "Job: Reverent in Suffering":

> The sobs of grief and pain are not the sign of unbelief. Job knows nothing of a flippant, insensitive, superficial "Praise God anyhow" response to suffering. The magnificence of his worship is because it was in grief,

not because it replaced grief. Let your tears flow freely when your calamity comes. And let the rest of us weep with those who weep.

In Job, we have the greatest man among all the peoples of the East now in the condition of being destitute, childless, and broken. He went from being the greatest to being the least. Yet because of God's faithful grace given to him, look at Job's response:

> Job got up and tore his robe and shaved his head. Then he fell to the ground in worship and said: "Naked I came from my mother's womb, and naked I will depart. The LORD gave and the LORD has taken away; may the name of the LORD be praised." (Job 1:20–21)

19

Lessons from a Horse Named Clyde

While Glenn was in the hospital, the doctor began going over Glenn's chart with me. He said there were other concerns he'd noticed in Glenn's CAT scan that were unrelated to his accident. He described them as "a malrotation and other birth-related issues." Glenn would need to see a pediatric gastroenterologist.

As the doctor exited the room, my eyes glanced over at Glenn lying in the hospital bed. The words of Romans 8:28 came to mind: "And we know that in all things God works for the good of those who love him, who have been called according to his purpose."

I didn't fully comprehend the medical terminology the doctor had used. But I felt the presence of God and believed He was working something good.

In Unknown Danger

Apparently, Glenn's organs had not developed properly while he was in the womb. Almost always children with this condition are treated within the first month of their lives, but Glenn's condition went undetected. If he hadn't had a CAT scan at the time of the trailer accident, we would never have been aware of his other health issues. Realizing this, I recalled holding Glenn's hand in the ambulance and praying Habakkuk 1:5—that God would do something utterly amazing.

Glenn would eventually be seen by a specialist at Johns Hopkins. We were told the situation in Glenn's intestines made him a "walking time bomb." Malrotation can cause health problems that are life-threatening.

Many times in life we're in danger and don't even know it! God was continuing to direct our lives and to place individuals and doctors into our path at just the right time.

As we visited with doctors and they reviewed Glenn's medical history, we realized Glenn had presented problems in the past that had gone undetected.

While the focus during this time was on Glenn, this event also deeply affected Briggs, as I was to discover later:

December 2

I picked up Briggs from school today. Just the two of us in the van. I tried to ask him about the happenings at school but he wasn't interested in chatting. Then out of the blue, he states, "Mom, when I close my eyes, I can see Glenn getting run over, over and over again."

His statement caught me so by surprise that I almost slammed on the brakes. I have been so concentrated on getting Glenn well and finishing my own 32 treatments that I haven't thought of how this has affected Briggs. I knew the accident was frightening for him. I know he was scared. I remembered his face when he came to see Glenn at the hospital and saw he was hooked up to the IVs and couldn't walk. It's a lot to take in when you are six years old and have been thrust into a very mature role during the past year. As a kindergartener he took on the role of a caregiver both physically and emotionally. Always helping Stan or whoever was staying with them. He had been so strong on so many levels that I had viewed him as older than he really was.

I pulled the van over into the church parking lot so we could talk. I turned around and looked into his hazel eyes and my heart hurt. The past year had certainly not gone as I had planned our picture-book life. One thing I had learned is that we cannot protect our children from pain and suffering as much as we would like to. Pain and suffering are part of the world we live in. Even when we try our best to make good decisions and do everything right, our life is not void of it. I lifted up a prayer in my mind, "Lord, help me know what to say to him."

I asked him to tell me what he saw when he closed his eyes. Little had been said about the accident since it happened. No one wanted to talk about it. Briggs began to relive the events of that sunny July afternoon out in the field. He focused on the fact that he was screaming, "STOP, STOP, STOP!" However, Brian could not hear his voice over the sound of the tractor. He ended with saying, "I saw the trailer go over Glenn's body and when I saw him lying in the grass, I thought Glenn was dead."

I put my hand on his arm and tell him I am sorry that he has that image in his mind. As I continue to gaze over his face, he is not emotional, just solemn. After the past year, I think Briggs is past the outward emotional stage. But he is clearly burdened. I tell him I don't understand why some things happen in life, but Daddy and I are focusing on the good things we see from Glenn's accident. Even though he had heard us discuss it before, I reminded him of the CT scan that revealed birth defects that we never knew existed. We discussed some of the issues that Glenn had experienced during the years that no one had an explanation for. Now, we know he has a problem that needs to be corrected. In life we must choose to focus on the good.

We talk about how good Glenn is doing and then out of nowhere Briggs announces, "I am ready for a snack."

A Young Boy's Love

My journal entries from several months later tell some of the story.

December 8

Stan's parents arrived to stay with Briggs while my mom, Stan, and I take Glenn to Baltimore for surgery.

I will never forget the scene as we left the house this morning. Briggs was getting ready for school. I sense deep down he wants to go with us; moreover, Glenn doesn't want to leave him.

I realize all three of his family members are leaving headed to the hospital; this time Briggs is the only one left behind.

As we say our goodbyes, Glenn starts to cry. Tears

stream down his face. I try to console him, but he doesn't want me. He just hugs Briggs. A picture of deep brotherly love and comfort.

Because I have been absent, I have not realized that during the course of the past fourteen months, my sons have been each other's comfort. Stability. Security.

Briggs doesn't cry—instead he just pats Glenn on the back and tells him, "It will be okay, buddy. Everything will be okay."

December 9

Johns Hopkins Hospital, pediatric waiting room. Glenn's hand clasped in mine.

They place him on the operating table. The mask is placed over his face. His arms begin to jerk, and his eyes roll back into his head. Slowly, he drifts off into the world of anesthesia.

Here I am, sitting in the waiting room full of other anxious moms and dads. I look down at the two little brown eyes belonging to Clyde, Glenn's stuffed horse. I laugh at the friends our children choose. Clyde—or as Glenn fondly refers to him, "my bust friend"—resurfaced in our life about six weeks ago. The day had come to clean out Glenn's closet. Who knows what had accumulated there during the past year? I strategically planned to tackle this task while Glenn was away.

As I sorted through the sea of toys, stuffed animals, and McDonald's giveaways, I began to make two piles: one of items to keep, and the other to give away. Clyde

was on his way to a Goodwill organization. Until...
Glenn came bursting in the door and caught a glimpse
of him. What a reunion!

Since that day, Clyde's been with us everywhere. I've
buckled him into a car seat, kissed him goodnight,
tiptoed around the house during his pretend naps, etc.

And here we sit in the hospital waiting room today.
Me and Clyde, my comforting companion.

Clyde came into our family when Glenn was about
sixteen months old, during Vacation Bible School.
Our church has a store where kids can buy new and
some slightly used toys with "bucks" they earn for
saying their memory verses, bringing friends, etc.

Glenn chose Clyde. Lucky for Glenn, he was my second
child. I would never have allowed my firstborn to bring
home a germ-inhabited "used stuffed animal."

Since Clyde's arrival into the Parris home, I've often
tossed him to the back of the closet or placed him in
a big plastic tub. Of all the great stuffed animals that
Glenn has, why would he choose Clyde?

Funny, which friends in life become our most cher-
ished relationships. This year I am thankful for the
Clydes in my life.

But most of all, I'm thankful for Christ. Of all the
things he could have chosen, he chose *me*—even when
at times I tossed Him into the back of my closet.

An email to family and friends:

January 15

To my partners in prayer:

Many of you have called and emailed us concerning our son, Glenn. We took him back to Johns Hopkins last week for his follow-up checkup after his surgery in December. The doctors were *very* pleased with the surgery and his recovery. So much so that he will not have to return unless a problem arises!

Once again we found God's favor resting on our shoulders.

Thank you for your faithful prayers. We can never put into words what that meant to us, except to say I count you all my *Clydes!*

Love,

Susan

20

To Caretakers: A Guide from My Husband, Stan

We've been on an amazing journey. You've been with me as I revealed each step of the way, from the first time I noticed something was wrong, the options for treatment, through my various challenges, and listening to me talk about Briggs and Glenn. You've heard me tell you how remarkable Stan has been throughout this ordeal. His love and support helped me in ways that cannot be measured, while he offered me hope and the willpower to continue. I asked him to share with you some of his thoughts and feelings from the viewpoint of the caretaker.

Susan and I left Southwestern Baptist Theological Seminary in Fort Worth, Texas, with high hopes, a good work ethic, and a love for God and each other. Everything else we had we could put in the smallest U-Haul truck you could rent. We made the long drive from Fort Worth to Vansant, Virginia, to begin our ministry together.

As the newly called pastor, I quickly realized I had no idea what

I was doing. In fact, my first Christmas I received as a gift a book titled *Everything You Need to Know that They Didn't Teach You in Seminary*. It seemed like a subtle hint regarding what I'd already feared! Thankfully, my church family was patient and overlooked my failures and flaws and found a way to love me.

What neither seminary or a book could teach me was the reality of pain and the scars that life would bring to many in my congregation. Life hurts. Pain is real. People suffer. In the first few years of my ministry, I conducted a funeral for a stillborn child and a sixteen year old killed in a car wreck. I led a community memorial service for three people murdered in a school shooting. I noticed that no one is immune to the pains of life. I always prayed that my heart wouldn't grow cold toward the pain I was seeing all around me.

God allowed me to sense pain and grief in a very personal way when my wife was diagnosed with cancer in October 2004, and again when my son was injured in July 2005. Compassion became more than a job. Because of these experiences, providing care to someone hurting became *personal* for me. I recall waiting in the holding area with Susan at MD Anderson Cancer Center, longing for someone who was close to God to come and pray with us before her surgery.

As a caretaker, you play a unique role. You show your love to your spouse; you constantly affirm that things are improving; you work out the details of appointments and travel; you answer the countless questions of "How is she doing?"; you put on a determined front when the doctor gives you bad news; you take care of the children; you become the primary housekeeper; and you try to fulfill your obligations at work. Outside these responsibilities, you have a lot of free time!

I thought it would be important to share some insights that I learned from cancer, the great teacher.

1. Let others help you.

The Lone Ranger approach to cancer doesn't work. I'm an independent, headstrong, do-it-yourself kind of man. Yet the relentless demands that cancer puts on a family forced my hand.

If someone offers, let them help you. You'll be blessed, and they'll get a blessing in helping you. I'll discuss in a moment the need to say no, but there are also times when you need to say yes.

2. Be positive, but honest.

A positive attitude is an essential part of the cancer battle. Paul tells us in Philippians 1:27, "Whatever happens, conduct yourselves in a manner worthy of the gospel of Christ." The cancer patient will have good days and bad days. The caregiver will have good days and bad days. However, it's important to maintain a positive attitude and be encouraging.

At the same time, it's important to be honest about the situation. While being positive, the caregiver should also be careful not to alter the reality. Whatever the truth is, God will give you the faith to deal with it.

3. Focus on getting well, not on the obstacles.

A key mistake many people make in their healthcare decisions is to let what they perceive as obstacles hinder them from making the best decision. Certainly, medical costs and traveling are incredibly expensive. Susan and I spent much of our savings on medical expenses, hotels, plane tickets, and food. However, you shouldn't let money determine your decision making. The stakes are too high to be consumed with the expenses.

Susan and I were blessed with friends and family who supported us financially on our cancer journey. Also, we sacrificed other things so we could travel and get the medical care Susan needed. There's no doubt that God blessed us and provided what we needed.

4. Be disciplined physically and spiritually.

During Susan's cancer journey, I made a terrible mistake. I didn't take care of myself physically. I was flying to Houston more than thirty flights in a year, driving frequently from Virginia to North Carolina, and trying to maintain my job and to deal with our young sons. Meanwhile I wasn't exercising or eating healthy. This took a toll on me, and it took years to recover. As hard as it can be, it's important that you discipline yourself to stay physically healthy.

The Bible says there's some good in bodily discipline—but it's an *essential* that you discipline yourself spiritually. You'll be on an emotional roller coaster. At times it will seem like the appointments, bad news, sickness, chemotherapy, and stress will never end. *You need God.*

People would often ask me if I was bitter that God allowed this to happen to my wife, especially since I was a pastor. I would respond, "Are you kidding? I'm not running from God; I am running *to* Him."

Spend time with God every day. Pray. Read your Bible. Praise God.

5. Take a break from time-consuming people and activities.

During these difficult times, you have a great opportunity to say no. Take advantage of it. There will be people who want to insert themselves into what's going on in your life. Some people love drama and love to become part of the story. And some people are just nosy. To be honest, they don't really care about you that much; they're interested in knowing information so they can be the first to share and get attention for it. When your loved one has cancer, you have a great opportunity to say no to such people.

Susan often joked that when she was battling cancer, she felt the least amount of stress in her life. Why? She had permission to say no.

You cannot afford to waste your physical and emotional energy on people and activities that are stressful and draining.

While most people have good intentions, some don't have the emotional intelligence to understand when it's time to leave or end the call on the phone. Don't feel bad about confronting these people. Doing it early will save you a lot of stress on the journey.

6. Be an advocate for your spouse.

Seek excellence from everyone involved with your spouse's care.

Susan was receiving medical treatment from some of the most renowned doctors and hospitals in the world. Yet, on several occasions we discovered mistakes. For instance, it was my job before every chemotherapy treatment to look at the doctor's orders and ask the nurse to read to me what was in the bag. On at least two occasions, the bag contained the wrong medicine or wrong amount. Mistakes happen at hospitals all across the country with serious consequences. It's essential that you watch carefully what's happening to your loved one.

I would spend hours on the Internet researching possible treatment plans and the latest information available on breast-cancer drugs. Doctors and nurses are under a lot of pressure. They're overworked and often taken for granted. Therefore, like all of us, they make mistakes. Your job is to be aware, ask questions, take notes, and speak up for your loved one—who will often be too sick, tired, or depressed to speak up for herself.

7. Pray.

You have two options on this journey. You can go through it alone. Or you can go through it with God.

Your connection to God is prayer. What a great resource you have to talk to the God of the universe, who knit together your loved one's body! He loves you and your loved one—and He's the Great Physician.

8. Journal and take pictures.

Susan and I weren't very good at taking photographs during this time. Susan didn't want the boys to remember her looking sick. Yet now, as we look back, we wish that we'd chronicled our journey with more pictures. The few we have are a great reminder to us of what we've been through, how God was working in our lives, and what God has done for us.

Susan did a great job of writing during her sickness. This book grew out of her journal entries. On the other hand, I did a terrible job of writing. I wish now I could go back and read what God was saying to me each day, and how He was leading me through the entire process.

9. Don't make it about you.

It's easy to have a pity party about how hard your life is. Being a caregiver is a huge burden, one that's impossible to understand unless you've been there. Yet your loved one *needs* this support from you, and it's essential that you don't try to usurp the attention toward yourself. Although such attention might feel good and right, it's not healthy for you, for your loved one, or for the healing process.

Find trusted friends and vent when you need too. Otherwise, focus on God and on your loved one getting well.

10. Celebrate the small things.

When you or someone you love has cancer, small things have a lot of meaning. As you go through your journey, take the time to celebrate, even if it seems small. Susan and I would celebrate when she left the hospital, knowing that at any moment she would be going back. Yet for the moment, it felt good. Rejoice and praise God for each answered prayer, and He'll use that praise to encourage you, renew your faith, and increase your hope.

I was recently traveling from North Carolina to my home in Virginia, a drive of four-and-a-half hours. It was a few days after Christmas, and Susan and the boys had decided to stay at her parents' house for a few extra days while I went back for work and to get ready for the following Sunday at church. During this drive I was having a pity party. Now, grant it, things weren't that bad, and certainly they could have been worse. But I was taking advantage of the "alone" time to voice my concerns to God about His handling of my life and especially about other things I wanted to happen—and happen *now*.

On this day, during this particular conversation, I sensed God speaking to me as never before. It was as if He said, "Okay, Stan, how many times do I have to go over this with you?"

I looked out the window and noticed the most beautiful rainbow I'd ever seen. The colors were magnificent. The rainbow looked like it was a complete circle.

About a half hour later, I looked out my car window and noticed a second rainbow.

Finally, after seeing *four* rainbows during a three-hour period—I surrendered. *Okay, God—as slow as I am, I think I get it. I can trust in Your promises!*

Cancer is a great teacher, but God is the ultimate promise keeper.

> And God said, "This is the sign of the covenant I am making between me and you and every living creature with you, a covenant for all generations to come: I have set my rainbow in the clouds, and it will be a sign of the covenant between me and the earth." (Genesis 9:12–13)

21

Power of One

One. The power of one is often underestimated. Yet, one person can make a tremendous difference.

For example, in 1948 just one additional vote in each precinct would have elected Thomas Dewey as president of the United States. In 1960, one vote in each precinct in Illinois would have elected Richard Nixon as president. Thomas Jefferson was elected president by one vote in the Electoral College. Rutherford B. Hayes was elected president by one vote. The Draft Act of World War II passed the House by one vote. One vote gave statehood to California, Idaho, Oregon, Texas, and Washington.

One is powerful.

The Bible is filled with examples of the power of one. One serpent deceived the first young couple on the planet, and we're all still dealing with the consequences. One man, Noah, and his family were found to be righteous and were spared the wrath of God through the ark. One man, Abram, was called by God to leave his home and become the leader of the nations. One woman, Rahab the prostitute, believed God and helped Israel conquer Jericho. One man, Nehemiah, had a calling in his life to rebuild the walls around Jerusalem, and the glory of the Lord was brought back to God's city. One woman, Ruth, refused to give up as she believed in the sovereign power of God. One prophet, Jeremiah, kept preaching the word of God even though no one was listening. One preacher, Jonah, got right with God and a whole city got saved. One couple, Mary and Joseph, accepted God's plan to redeem the world. One man, Stephen, stood his ground and kept the faith even as he was put to death. One criminal, hanging on a cross beside that of Jesus, became a believer and found himself in paradise. One man, Peter, had faith and kept his eyes on Jesus and was able to walk on water.

And one Man, one God—Jesus—died as our redeeming sacrifice on the cross, a death that was sufficient for the sins of the world.

There is power in one.

Reaping What You Sow

I often think about the power of one in my own life. I've learned the principle that one seed can grow rich harvests. I sow in one season, I reap in another.

I grew up on a family farm. You plant in the spring, and you harvest in the fall. Every farmer knows this. It's also a principle from God that proves true in our spiritual lives. God encourages us, "Let us not become weary in doing good, for at the proper time we will reap a harvest if we do not give up" (Galatians 6:9).

I found this principle to be true: When I was willing to sow one act of obedience, God demonstrated how He could use it to bring a harvest.

As I was growing up, our church was always actively involved in missions. I can't remember a Christmas when the Lottie Moon Christmas Offering wasn't a part of my life. Lottie Moon was a missionary to China who literally gave her life to the service of the gospel there. In her memory, Baptist churches have established an offering at Christmas for missions around the world.

The first Christmas after Stan and I were married, we made a commitment that regardless of our financial situation, we would give each year to the Lottie Moon Christmas Offering for missions. And for our first Christmas together, that mission offering was the biggest Christmas gift we gave.

A seed was planted. I never imagined then, at the age of twenty-two, how that would play out in my life.

One Who Made a Difference for Me

Throughout my journey, I've witnessed the power of one. God made sure I understood the power of one when I met a nurse named Nette. I mentioned her previously because she gave me a book that had an important message about "love heals." Through her, God revealed to me that one person can make a difference.

On November 12, 2004, I was in Houston, sick and alone. Stan had gone home to preach. I'd gotten an infection and was in the hospital. The nurse came in to take my vitals, and while she was treating me she asked, "Are you a Christian?"

I responded, "Yes."

She then proceeded across the room and shut my door. She came over to my bed and got down on her knees. She took my hand and placed it between hers. Then, in her broken English, she prayed that God would heal my body. It was one of the most beautiful and powerful prayers I've ever heard.

When Nette found out I was a Baptist pastor's wife, she treated me like royalty. Her care was unsurpassed. On her day off, she even walked to the hospital (having no other means of transportation) to care for me.

Nette didn't grow up knowing about Jesus. But when she was a young woman, a Baptist missionary came to her village and told her about Jesus and His saving power. She accepted Him as her Lord and Savior, as did many of her family members.

Nette had been in the United States only two months when we met that November day. Here was a Baptist minister's wife sick and alone, 1,000 miles from her family and friends, in a hospital with 18,000 employees. On that day, I was assigned to a room, and Nette was assigned to care for me. There is power in one.

Only *God* orchestrates these encounters in our lives.

Our Lottie Moon offering, along with many others in Baptist churches across this country, went to a missionary in the Philippines who went to a village where the people didn't know about Christ. The missionary shared with them the Word of God. There is power in one. They responded in faith. And lives, like Nette's, were changed for eternity. The power of one.

I'd become the recipient of my very own gift. What we sow in one season, we reap in another.

Nette would go on to take care of me for the next six months. I would meet her in the infusion center several times a week, and she would clean my CVC line to keep me free from infection. I'll always credit her care and God's grace for how amazed the doctors were at the condition of the CVC line inserted into my shoulder for more than thirteen months.

Nette not only took care of me physically, but she was a bright spot in my day. Her hugs and sacrifices made me feel loved. She diligently prayed for the healing of my body. Even though she'd lost her only child, she prayed faithfully for my two boys. She encouraged me through Scripture and brought me books to read.

She was a gift that came into my life unexpectedly. A gift no amount of money could ever buy. Heaven sent. *The power of one.*

22

A Final Word: He Loves Me

He loves me…he loves me not….

As a kid, I enjoyed lazy afternoons lying in the fields plucking petals off daisies. I would bask in the wonderment of love and sunshine. Feeling loved always brought a euphoric rush to my soul.

He loves me, he loves me not… If I ended on "he loves me not," I simply picked another daisy and started over. If only life could be that simple! We could change outcomes by simply picking another daisy and trying again. Cancer could be benign. Broken relationships fixed. Words erased. Love reciprocated.

Our petal-picking rhyme gets more serious with age and life experiences. As I talk with people going through the storms of life, I often hear the question, "Does God love me? Does God care about my pain?"

The questioning of God comes from the new wave of thinking that has swept the American religious landscape. The thinking goes something like this: *If I do my part, if I'm a relatively good person, I can expect God to do His part and provide me with a comfortable life. After all, if I'm good, God owes me.*

The problem here is that God does *not* owe me. In fact, there aren't enough good things I could ever do to put God in a position of being indebted to me. The all-powerful, all-knowing, holy and righteous God is a God of grace. He *allows* me to know Him. He *allows* me into His presence. There's nothing I can do on my own to change the fact that I'm a sinful and rebellious created being. But by the invitation of God, I'm offered His forgiveness and hope, and by faith I trust Him to navigate my life according to His sovereign plan.

Yet we all know that such a life is not for the faint of heart. "Living by faith is a bewildering venture," Eugene Peterson, author of *The Message: The Bible in Contemporary Language*, writes. "We rarely know what's coming next, and not many things turn out the way we anticipate."

The questioning of God did not start with our generation. The book of Habakkuk took place in the seventh century B.C. This small book of three chapters begins with Habakkuk boldly asking God some of the same questions we have today:

"How long, LORD, must I call for help, but you do not listen?" (Habakkuk 1:2)

"Why do you make me look at injustice?" (Habakkuk 1:3)

"Why do you tolerate wrongdoing?" (Habakkuk 1:3)

Habakkuk was impatient and frustrated. He wondered why God allowed injustice and evil to continue unpunished. His words jump off the page like a modern-day blog. *Why does it seem like God isn't answering my prayers? Why is it those who do evil seem to flourish? Life isn't fair!*

God's response to such questioning from Habakkuk was shocking and confusing. God said, "I am raising up the Babylonians, that ruthless and impetuous people, who sweep across the whole earth to seize dwelling places not their own" (Habakkuk 1:6).

What? God explained that he would use the Babylonians, a

godless people, to conquer Judah, the chosen nation. But how could God use a nation more wicked than Judah to punish them?

Is God unfair, unconcerned? What's the deal here?

I think that's how Habakkuk felt—and how *we* feel during the storms of life.

What Habakkuk said next is something I found so critical in my own journey: "I will stand at my watch and station myself on the ramparts; I will look to see what he will say to me, and what answer I am to give to this complaint" (Habakkuk 2:1).

Habakkuk was a wise man. He decided to wait, listen, and pray. And so must we.

We don't know how long it took for God to answer Habakkuk. It might have been days, months, or years. Sometimes our impatience makes us think that God doesn't care. Yet He's always on time—His time.

In the end, God tells Habakkuk that evil will *not* triumph over good. God is sovereign. Habakkuk's circumstances didn't change, but his encounter with God changed *him*. Wow! That's truly better than picking another daisy.

This profound outcome for Habakkuk has been summarized by Eugene Peterson in these words: "Only there did he eventually realize that the believing-in-God life, the steady trusting-in-God life, is the full life, the only life. Habakkuk started out exactly where we start out with our puzzled complaints and God accusations, but he didn't stay there. He ended up in a world, along with us, where every detail in our lives of love for God is worked into something good."

Habakkuk began with questions, but didn't stay there. We can't stay there either, if we're to survive life's storms with a healthy soul. By faith, we trust in God's plan for our lives, and we trust God's timing.

One of the saddest verses in the Bible, to me, is this one:

> Time and again they pushed him to the limit, pro-
> voked Israel's Holy God. How quickly they forgot
> what he'd done, forgot their day of rescue from the
> enemy. (Psalm 78:41–42, *The Message*).

The Israelites had witnessed the power of God in dramatic ways. They'd seen God devastate the Egyptians with ten plagues. They'd seen God destroy and drown Pharaoh's chariots and horses at the Red Sea. They'd seen God supernaturally provide them with meat, manna, and water in the wilderness. They'd seen God lead them through the desert and keep them warm with a pillar of fire. Yet after all this, when God instructed them to go into the Promised Land, they refused. Why? *They didn't trust Him.*

Oh, sure, they faced significant challenges in that land. Giants were there, and fortified cities, and armies with powerful weapons. Obstacles were certainly before them.

But instead of trusting the God who sent the ten plagues, who inundated Pharaoh's army, who created and kept aflame the pillar of fire—God's people doubted Him and refused to go forward. They didn't trust His plan, and His timing looked terrible.

But God always has an appointed time for His plans. Throughout the Bible, we see Him working out His plan on His own timetable. God had an appointed time to show up at the tomb of Lazarus—when everybody thought He was too late—and to raise Lazarus from the dead. God had an appointed time for Sarah to become pregnant, though Sarah was so unsure of it that she laughed at the very idea. God had an appointed time to put Paul in prison so he could write a large portion of the New Testament.

And God has an appointed time for every detail of your life and mine.

> "For my thoughts are not your thoughts, neither are your ways my ways," declares the LORD. "As the heavens are higher than the earth, so are my ways higher than your ways and my thoughts than your thoughts." (Isaiah 55:8–9)

This means God has a perfect plan for your life—and His perfect timing comes with it. If we want to see God's greatest blessings in our lives, we must be willing to wait not only on the plan but also on the timing.

I have to believe this is true. Because if life is only random—a bunch of random acts having no meaning or purpose—then what's the point of living? If my cancer was the result of random bad luck, I'm ready to go hide in a cave and hope nothing worse happens to me.

Behind every one of my problems in life is not random chance or bad luck, but God's purpose. When I get this perspective on life, it changes everything.

In your life, maybe you feel there's some problem that keeps you from really living. You think, *If I could just change this circumstance, I could really live and be happy.* It's like you're in prison, chained to your problem.

Maybe it's your job. You're thinking, *If God would just get me out of this dead-end job and away from these annoying coworkers, I could be really happy. God, get me out!*

Or it could be a relationship. You feel chained to someone at work, in the neighborhood, in your church, or even in your family. This person is driving you crazy, sucking the life right out of you. You dread the sight of them, and try your best to avoid them.

It could also be an addiction you feel chained to—your own, or that of a loved one. *God, set me free!*

It might be a huge debt or some other financial burden. I know a couple in my church who were trying for nearly four years to sell their house. It was like an albatross around their neck. They were chained to a mortgage and could find no way out. They were sure that once they got get rid of that house, life would be happy again.

In any of those situations, we tend to ask God the same questions Habakkuk was asking. *God, why are You allowing this to happen to me? Why do I feel like I'm in prison, chained to my circumstances, and You aren't helping? Don't You want me to be happy?*

For me, I felt like I was chained to a body that was broken. Thirty-four years old, and I had cancer. How did this happen?

I'm supposed to be enjoying life, spending time with my two kids and living a happy, soccer-mom life. After all, I've been good. I go to church. I even married the pastor! I've always given money to the special offering for missionaries.

This is not fair!

God answered my questions. He doesn't always do that; He's not obligated to answer our questions. But one day God's voice spoke to my soul: *Could it be I have allowed you to be chained to this body so I can be glorified through you?*

Maybe that annoying, needy person you feel chained to is someone God wants to show His love to through you. Maybe you have an addicted child or a house that won't sell because this represents your greatest opportunity to glorify God and to show how your trust is really in Him.

When God answered me, He also reminded me that just as His plans and His timing are perfect, so also He is sovereign over anything that we might feel chained to. Something Stan experienced really brought this truth home.

I've heard Stan recount the following story several times. We were in Houston; I'd just been released from the hospital, and we were staying that night in a hotel near the hospital. Then I started running a fever.

Listen to Stan tell the story:

> *No Tylenol.* That was my job; I was supposed to have Tylenol.
>
> By now it was 11:30 at night. Nothing open close by. *What am I going to do?*
>
> I called a taxi, then went down in front of the hotel and waited for it. The taxi pulled up, and I got in. It was smelly and dirty.
>
> I looked at the driver. He looked about twenty-five. He had a Mohawk with hair spiked up to the top of the car. His arms were sleeved in tattoos, and he had piercings on every part of his body that could possibly be pierced.
>
> He turned around and looked at me. "Where you going?"
>
> I wanted to say, "Back to my room," but I was on a mission. I told him to find the closest place where I could buy some Tylenol.
>
> He started driving. I think he took me into the meanest, most crime-ridden neighborhood in Houston's inner city, and we pulled up to a convenience store. I knew if I got out, I would never be seen again.
>
> But I was on a mission.
>
> "You better not leave," I told the driver, "or I will hunt you down. You don't want that to happen. I know what you look like."

I ran inside, found the Tylenol, and hustled back into the taxi. Then the Spirit of God spoke as clear as day: "Tell that boy about Jesus."

Not interested, God. Not interested in doing that right now.

But the Spirit of God was so powerful at that moment, I thought that if I didn't say something, I might not make it back.

From the back seat, I looked at the driver and said, "Have you ever heard about Jesus?"

Complete silence.

"Hey," I repeated, "have you ever heard about Jesus?"

Nothing.

Well, I thought, *I tried, Lord.*

I sensed the Spirit of God urging me simply to keep speaking of Jesus.

I leaned forward and explained the plan of salvation. "Jesus Christ loves you and has a plan for your life...." I went through the whole thing. I ended by saying, "I know you can hear me. Jesus Christ loves you."

We arrived back at the hotel; he still hadn't spoken a word in response.

I was thinking, *Lord, what a mess my life is right now. I'm down here with this totally unresponsive guy, my wife's in bed with cancer—what is going on?*

Then it happened. God said, "Stan, I put you here so you could speak to that taxi driver. He needs to hear that somebody loves him. And there are going to be others like him. This is your chance to bring Me glory."

That's when I knew that Susan and I were not chained to cancer; cancer had been chained to *us*—so that more people could hear that Jesus Christ loves them.

❧

Paul wrote the Book of Philippians while in a Roman prison, chained to a prison guard. The chain was probably no longer than eighteen inches. Can you imagine being chained that closely to another human being for twenty-four hours a day? No time alone. You couldn't move without that other person's cooperation. Yet we find in Philippians 1:16 one of the most powerful lines in the whole of Scripture, where Paul states, "I am put here for the defense of the gospel."

Those few words give us a picture of life. Take note how he expressed it: "I am *put* here...." Paul looks around at his prison, at his suffering, and he's declaring, *This is where God has placed me!*

God has greater plans for us than we have for ourselves. Do you believe that? You would think Paul's predicament would be a huge barrier to the advancement of the gospel—he was locked in a prison! But this is how God had planned the gospel's progress. He had greater plans for His apostle than Paul had for himself.

You see, as a follower of Jesus Christ, however much you feel imprisoned, you can know this: You are not chained to those difficulties; *they have been chained to you*, for God's good purpose.

And one day Jesus Christ will set you free!

He loves me...utterly amazing!

Look at the nations and watch—
and be utterly amazed.
For I am going to do something in your days
that you would not believe,
even if you were told.
(Habakkuk 1:5)

Fast Forward

Today, I am doing well and living in Rocky Mount, Virginia. It has been eleven years since my breast cancer diagnosis. I still go to Houston every six months for check-ups. Herceptin, one of the drugs in my clinical trial, is now considered one of the greatest breakthroughs in breast cancer treatment in the past 20 years. My children are now 16 and 14. Wow, time flies! While my cancer journey changed all of our lives in different ways, here is what time and experience has taught me:

1. Take care of your body.

I always tried to eat healthy and exercise. What I learned is that taking care of my body is a lot more. Statistics from The National Cancer Center show that 41 percent of Americans will get cancer in their lifetime. Today, I think more about what I eat and put into my body than ever before. Also, I get at least eight hours of sleep a night. I realize the impact of stress on my physical body and health. I try to manage stress and mental health in practical ways. I honor the body that God has given me. When in doubt, I drink lots and lots of water.

2. Spend your resources on the important things in life.

We live in a culture that tells us to spend our life acquiring money and material things. I have found that faith, family, and friends are the greatest assets you will ever acquire. Spend your resources on these three things. They will be rays of sunshine on the rainy days.

3. God is in control of the seasons of our lives.

Each has a purpose. God can draw good out of even the difficult seasons of life. Be mindful of the seeds you are planting in this season. For what you plant in one season, you will reap in another.

4. Be an advocate for your health.

Not all doctors and hospitals are the same. Growing up I had many different school teachers. Some were better than others. I learned more from the good teachers. I have found what is true in education is also true in healthcare. The difference is that in healthcare the stakes are much higher. Always consider second opinions. It's only time and money. Both of which are insignificant in comparison to one's health. I have found the words of financial counselor and author Larry Burkett to be true, "No medical doctor is really responsible for your health; *you* are responsible for your health. Doctors may help guide, give alternatives, advise, and administer whatever therapy you choose, but it's *your* body, and you must make the final decisions" (*Nothing to Fear: The Key to Cancer Survival*, Moody Publishers, 2004, 11-12).

5. Pray. Pray. Pray.

If for no other reason, it is physically healthy for you. I will never underestimate the power of my prayers and, more important, the prayers of others praying for me. It is scientifically proven. Doctors believe it. I have experienced it.

6. Make it a life habit to go to church weekly and be a part of a small group.

Life is meant to be lived out in community with others. I can't imagine weathering the storm of cancer or facing the giants in front of me without the support of my church family. Our parents and siblings were wonderful, but this battle required a larger army. Imagine people with different skills and resources joining you in the trenches of life. Trust me, you might be able to win the battle on your own, but the scars will be deeper and greater when you fight alone. I will forever have an abiding love for Vansant Baptist Church and a deep bond with those who stood in the trenches with me.

7. Each day is a gift.

Generations have been obsessed with how they can live longer. I have come to the realization that God is not as interested in how long we live, but what we do with the days we have been given. Spend today wisely. Love someone, for the power of love is a phenomenal thing.

8. Read the Bible every day.

Looking back, the one thing I am so grateful that I had planted in my life before my cancer diagnosis was God's Word. I have found it is the number one way God speaks to us. After my encounter with God and the book of Habakkuk, I realized the power of the Bible was far greater than I had ever imagined or understood. My life will never be the same. My prayer is that as I tell my story, you will also be changed and understand the POWER of the book that Christians base their eternity on, but seldom read.

Acknowledgments

In too many ways to enumerate, many people, named and unnamed, supported me throughout my cancer journey, and they continue to sustain me today. My gratitude to them is endless. I can only hope to pay it forward to others battling this disease.

To Franklin Heights Baptist Church and Vansant Baptist Church: Two communities of faith who continue to make a difference in the lives of others. Thank you.

To our families: Peggy and Bruce Briggs; Brian and Bradley Briggs; JoAnne and Jerry Parris; Stephen, Shawn, Chandler, and Cassie Parris; and Scott Parris—thank you for loving me, supporting me, and praying for me.

To Briggs and Glenn: I pray the words of this book will serve as a reminder to you of the power of God and His word. I love being your mom.

To Stan: Your sacrificial love made the journey possible. You are my best friend and a constant advocate for my health. Thank you for fighting for me. This book would have never happened without you. I count it a great blessing to be walking together with you on this journey called life. I love you *always*.

To Jesus: Thank you for the gift of life, both here on earth and in our eternal home in heaven. This is YOUR story.

About the Author

Susan Parris is a mother, pastor's wife, and cancer survivor. Born and raised in Waynesville, North Carolina, Susan and her family now reside in Virginia with their rescue dog, Turbo. Besides her role as mom and wife, Susan is vice president and marketing director of TruPoint Bank. She cheers for the University of Georgia, where she graduated cum laude.

You can connect with Susan on Facebook at www.facebook.com/CancerMombySusanParris

If you found this book to be helpful, will you consider sharing the message with others?

- Write a review on Amazon.com, bn.com, or Goodreads.

- Mention this book in a Facebook post, Twitter update, Pinterest pin, or blog post.

- Pick up a copy for someone you know who is battling cancer or has someone close battling this disease.

CPSIA information can be obtained
at www.ICGtesting.com
Printed in the USA
BVOW08s0248211216
471459BV00001B/240/P